CONCISE

Windows™ for Workgroups

Kris Jamsa

PUBLISHED BY
Microsoft Press
A Division of Microsoft Corporation
One Microsoft Way
Redmond, Washington 98052-6399

Library of Congress Cataloging-in-Publication Data

Jamsa, Kris A.
   Concise guide to windows for workgroups / Kris Jamsa.
      p.   cm.
   Includes index.
   ISBN 1-55615-505-0
   1. Microsoft Windows (Computer file) 2. Computer networks.
  I. Title.
  QA76.76.W56J3655   1992
  005.4'3--dc20   92-28319
                                                       CIP

Printed and bound in the United States of America.

1 2 3 4 5 6 7 8 9   AGAG   7 6 5 4 3 2

Distributed to the book trade in Canada by Macmillan of Canada, a division of Canada Publishing Corporation.

Distributed to the book trade outside the United States and Canada by Penguin Books Ltd.

Penguin Books Ltd., Harmondsworth, Middlesex, England
Penguin Books Australia Ltd., Ringwood, Victoria, Australia
Penguin Books N.Z. Ltd., 182-190 Wairau Road, Auckland 10, New Zealand

British Cataloging-in-Publication Data available.

Acquisitions Editor: Michael Halvorson
Project Editor: Ron Lamb
Technical Editor: Mary DeJong

Contents

Introduction

In 1981, IBM released its first personal computer, Microsoft released MS-DOS, and the PC revolution began. Throughout the 1980s, millions of users learned to issue a variety of MS-DOS commands and to use a variety of applications.

By the end of the decade, most users had a word processor, a spreadsheet, and possibly a database application they used regularly. In fact, most users were seeking an easy way to exchange information between applications—a method that would eliminate the need to close one application before looking up information stored by another.

In 1990, Microsoft introduced Windows 3.0, a program designed to maximize productivity. Windows 3.0 made computers easier to use, made applications easier to learn, and allowed several applications to run at the same time. And—perhaps more important—it provided a simple means of information exchange between applications. Windows provides menus, icons (meaningful symbols), and dialog boxes that replace the often cryptic commands that MS-DOS requires.

In 1992, Microsoft released Windows 3.1, which provides object links to help applications share data; TrueType fonts, which you can size to any height and print exactly as they appear on the screen; enhanced help; and even an online tutorial. Windows 3.1 brings multimedia to the PC world. If your PC has a sound board, a CD-ROM drive, and a MIDI device, Windows 3.1 provides you with the ability to record, edit, and play video and sounds. In addition, Windows 3.1 lets you assign specific sounds to various system events.

Also in 1992, Microsoft released a version of Windows called Windows for Workgroups, which allows a group of people to share information among their machines. Windows for Workgroups makes the exchange of messages and information among users in a workgroup as simple as a click of the mouse. It also maintains the icons and mouse interface of earlier versions of Windows that made the computer a natural extension of the user's desktop. From its scheduling utility to its use of electronic mail, shared directories, and object linking and embedding (OLE) between computers, Windows for Workgroups provides users with all the facilities they need to communicate and share data with other members of their workgroup.

Just as the 1980s saw the PC revolution, the 1990s are seeing the Windows revolution.

How to Use This Book

This book is bursting at the bindings with information you need to put Windows for Workgroups to use:

■ Part I defines the elements of a window and describes how to use them. It also introduces the extensive online help feature Windows provides.

■ Part II describes how to use the Program Manager to run applications. The Program Manager organizes applications into groups, simplifying the selection of related applications, such as a word processor and a spreadsheet. It also introduces the File Manager, which manages connections between computers, displays directory listings, and performs essential file operations such as Copy, Rename, and Delete, and describes how to use the PIF Editor and the ClipBook Viewer. Part II also describes the Print Manager, which controls printer sharing and output, and the Task List, which moves you quickly among running applications. Lastly, Part II describes Mail and Schedule+.

■ Part III explains how to customize Windows according to hardware needs (printer types, port usage, and network type) and personal preference (window colors, keyboard speed, cursor blink rate, and so on).

■ Part IV introduces the *desktop accessories* available with Windows — powerful programs that perform like many of the items commonly found on your desk, such as a clock, a notepad, a calculator, and an address book.

■ Part V introduces the Windows games Solitaire and Minesweeper.

Two appendixes provide you with special information:

■ Appendix A walks you through installing Windows for Workgroups.

■ Appendix B provides an easy-to-read list of keyboard shortcuts used within Windows.

In short, this reference contains all the steps you need to take, not just to get Windows started, but to really put Windows to work.

PART I

Essential Operations

This book assumes that Microsoft Windows for Workgroups is installed on your computer and that you're ready to start it and become acquainted with the basics of Windows. If it is not yet installed on your computer, you can get all the installation information you need by turning to Appendix A, "Installing Windows for Workgroups."

STARTING WINDOWS

To start Windows, type the following command at the MS-DOS prompt (C:\>), pressing Enter as shown:

```
WIN <Enter>
```

Windows first displays the Welcome to Windows for Workgroups dialog box shown in Figure 1-1.

FIGURE 1-1. *The Welcome to Windows for Workgroups dialog box.*

Type in the user name and password that you chose when you installed Windows for Workgroups. After you log on, you will be able to access any computer in your workgroup. A *workgroup* is a collection of computers that are connected by a network.

Windows for Workgroups lets you connect to printers and directories that reside on other computers. After you log onto the network, Windows attempts to connect to any remote resource you specified in a previous session. If you have directed Windows to connect to a remote resource and the computer possessing the resource is not currently running Windows, the connection will fail. Windows will display a dialog box describing the failure, prompting you to specify whether you want it to continue making other remote connections. In most cases, you will want Windows to make other connections, so choose Yes.

The Windows *desktop,* similar to Figure 1-2, then appears on your screen. To quickly learn the basics of Windows, you can run the online tutorial, as described later in Part I.

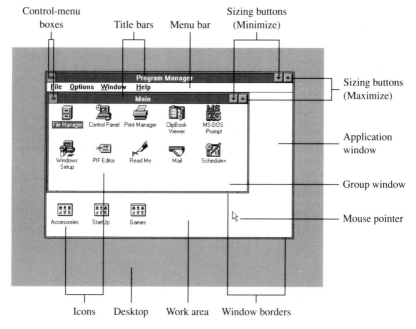

FIGURE 1-2. *After you start Windows, your screen looks something like this.*

WINDOWS AT A GLANCE

A *window* is simply a framed region on the screen. Each window contains the following elements (as shown in Figure 1-2):

■ *Window borders* are the four edges that define the window's region.

■ The *title bar* is the area directly below the window's top border. The title bar displays the window's name.

■ The *Control-menu box* is in the upper left corner of the window and has an inner rectangle.

■ The *mouse pointer* indicates where the mouse is currently positioned on the screen.

■ *Sizing buttons (Minimize/Maximize)* are buttons in the upper right corner of the window that minimize or maximize the window.

■ The *menu bar* is the area below the title bar. The menu bar provides access to most of an application's commands.

■ The *work area* is the area inside a window.

■ *Icons* are visual representations of minimized windows, applications, or documents.

Getting Around the Screen: A Primer

This book describes a variety of basic operations you can do in Windows. All can be carried out either with a mouse or from the keyboard. A mouse is strongly recommended, however, so the instructions in this book focus on the mouse.

Mouse users should know how to perform the following actions. (Typical uses for these actions are noted in parentheses.)

To click	Position the tip of the mouse pointer over the specified element, and then press and release the left mouse button one time. (Selecting windows, icons, or files; selecting dialog box options.)
To double-click	Position the tip of the mouse pointer over the specified element, and then press and release the left mouse button twice in quick succession without moving the mouse. (Expanding icons; executing applications; choosing items from a list.)
To drag	Position the tip of the mouse pointer over the specified element, hold down the left mouse button, and move the mouse. The mouse pointer moves, dragging the element. Move the element to the desired location and release the left mouse button. (Moving windows or icons; resizing windows.)

Keyboard users should know how to use *keyboard shortcuts*. A keyboard shortcut is a single keystroke or a combination of keystrokes that executes a command directly. For example, the keyboard shortcut Ctrl+F4 (which means press and hold down the Ctrl key while you press F4) provides the same result as choosing Close from the Control menu of the Main group window. Appendix B, "Fundamental Keys in Windows," lists the keyboard shortcuts for a variety of tasks.

Windows supports three kinds of windows. Two of them are *application windows* and subwindows within application windows (the latter are called *document windows*). Windows also supports a special type of document window called a *group window*, which contains application icons. In Figure 1-2, Program Manager is an application window, and Main is a group window. Also note the File Manager application icon, which is highlighted.

WORKING WITH ICONS

As shown in Figure 1-2, when you start Windows, a number of icons (graphical symbols of an application or a minimized window) appear. To work with an icon, you expand it—that is, you cause the icon to become a window residing on the desktop.

To expand an icon, double-click on the icon.

SELECTING A WINDOW

When your screen contains several application windows, you can select the one you want by clicking in the window or by repeatedly pressing Alt+Esc. You can tell when a window is selected because its borders and title bar darken. You can also select a window by holding down the Alt key and pressing Tab repeatedly. When the name of the window you want to use appears in the box in the middle of the screen, select it by releasing the Alt key.

WORKING WITH MENUS

Immediately below an application window's title bar is a menu bar. The menu bar lists the names of one or more *menus* (lists of related commands). For example, the Program Manager menu bar contains the File, Options, Window, and Help menus.

Opening a Menu

To open a menu, click on the menu name. When you open a menu, a list of *commands* appears, as shown in Figure 1-3.

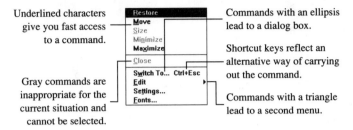

Underlined characters give you fast access to a command.

Commands with an ellipsis lead to a dialog box.

Shortcut keys reflect an alternative way of carrying out the command.

Gray commands are inappropriate for the current situation and cannot be selected.

Commands with a triangle lead to a second menu.

FIGURE 1-3. *A sample open menu.*

Selecting a Command

To select a command from a command menu, click on the command name or press the letter underlined in the command name.

Closing a Menu

To close a menu without selecting a command, click on a location outside of the menu, or press the Esc key.

WORKING WITH DIALOG BOXES

A *dialog box* is a window that frequently provides information and always requests a user response. Figure 1-4 shows a sample dialog box that helps you set up your desktop. A dialog box might simply display a

Drop-down list
(not dropped down)

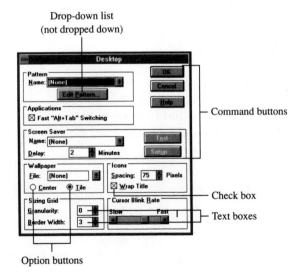

Command buttons

Check box

Text boxes

Option buttons

FIGURE 1-4. *A sample dialog box.*

status message, waiting until you select OK, or it might ask you to specify a filename or other information.

Dialog boxes can contain several fields of information, as described in the following paragraphs. To select a field, click on the desired field or press Alt+*X*, where *X* is the letter underlined in the field name.

Command buttons A command button directs a dialog box to perform a specific action.

Text box A text box lets you type in a text string, such as a filename. Sometimes a text box contains default text (which might be highlighted). To enter different text, simply type in the new text, which replaces the old text automatically. To make minor changes to the default text, press the left arrow key, and edit the text. As you edit, you can use the Backspace, Delete, and arrow keys.

List box A list box provides you with a list of options. If the list contains more options than the box can display, the box contains a scroll bar. To choose an option, click on the option. Double-click on the option if you want to select the option and close the dialog box. If the list lets you select multiple options, check the documentation that came with the application for instructions on selecting more than one.

Drop-down list Dialog boxes use drop-down lists when there's not enough room for a list box. Figure 1-5 shows a sample dialog box with a drop-down list. To drop the list down, click on the downward-pointing arrow at the right of the list.

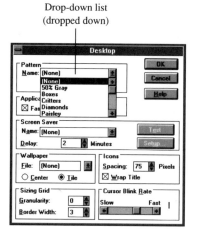

FIGURE 1-5. *A dialog box with a dropped-down list.*

Option button When the options you can select from are mutually exclusive—that is, when you are allowed to select only one of them at a time—they are grouped together as *option buttons*. Option buttons appear as circles with text next to them. One option in each group (the currently selected option) has a black dot in its center. Gray or dimmed options are inappropriate for the current situation; you cannot select them. To select an option button, click on the option button or its text.

Check box Options that you can turn on or off individually are displayed as check boxes. When a check box is empty, the option is not selected (off). An X in the check box indicates that the option is selected. Gray or dimmed options are inappropriate for the current situation and cannot be selected. To select or deselect a check box, click on the check box or its text.

SCROLLING FOR INFORMATION

When an application contains more information than can fit in a window, vertical and horizontal scroll bars appear along the window's right and bottom edges, as shown in Figure 1-6. Within each scroll bar, a *scroll box* moves to reflect your relative position within the document. To use scroll bars, follow these steps:

■ To move a short distance, click on the up and down or left and right arrows at each end of the scroll bar.

■ To move up by approximately one screen, click on the vertical scroll bar above the scroll box. To move down by approximately one screen, click on the vertical scroll bar below the scroll box. To move to the left by approximately one screen, click on the horizontal scroll bar to the left of the scroll box. To move to the right by approximately one screen, click on the horizontal scroll bar to the right of the scroll box.

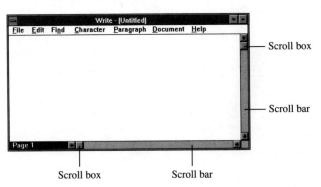

FIGURE 1-6. *Scroll bars and scroll boxes help you navigate within your document.*

■ To move to a specific location, drag the scroll box along the scroll bar.

SIZING A WINDOW

Windows provides you with several ways to increase or decrease the size of a window.

Minimizing a Window

To minimize a window—that is, to reduce it to an icon—click on the Minimize button (a downward-pointing triangle) in the upper right corner of the window.

Restoring a Minimized Window

To restore a minimized window—that is, to expand an icon to a window—double-click on the icon.

Maximizing a Window

To maximize a window—that is, to enlarge it to the fullest possible size—click on the Maximize button (an upward-pointing triangle) in the upper right corner of the window.

Restoring a Maximized Window

When you maximize a window, that window's Maximize button becomes a Restore button. To restore a window to its previous size, click on the Restore button (an upward-pointing triangle sitting on top of a downward-pointing triangle).

Incrementally Sizing a Window

To stretch or compress a window, drag a window border to the desired size. When you release the mouse button, Windows expands or shrinks the window to fill the new area.

■ To change window height, drag the window's top or bottom border.

■ To change window width, drag the window's left or right border.

■ To change both the height and the width, drag a corner where two borders meet.

MOVING A WINDOW

One of the benefits of the Windows desktop is that it allows you to move your work around to suit your needs and priorities. To move a window, drag the title bar of the window to the desired location.

NOTE: *When you move a window, Windows moves only an outline of the window until you release the mouse button.*

CLOSING A WINDOW

When you close an application window, the corresponding application stops running. If you have made changes and have not yet saved the changes on disk, a dialog box appears asking whether you want to save the changes.

To close a window, double-click on the window's Control-menu box.

USING THE CONTROL MENU

Every window has a *Control menu*, which contains commands that let you move, size, or close a window by using the keyboard (Figure 1-7).

FIGURE 1-7. *A typical Control menu.*

To open the Control menu, click on the Control-menu box in the window's upper left corner adjacent to the menu bar.

The following list briefly describes each Control-menu command:

Command	Function
Restore	Restores a window to its previous size following a minimize or maximize operation
Move	Lets you move the window using the arrow keys
Size	Lets you change the window's size using the arrow keys
Minimize	Reduces the window to an icon
Maximize	Expands the window to full size

(continued)

continued

Command	Function
Close	Closes the window
Switch To	Opens the Task List dialog box, which lets you select another running application
Next	Selects the next open document or group window within an application window

RUNNING THE ONLINE TUTORIAL

Windows for Workgroups provides an online tutorial that teaches you how to use a mouse with Windows. It also provides a lesson on the basics of how to use Windows. To run the tutorial, choose Windows Tutorial from the Program Manager's Help menu.

The tutorial displays a series of windows, each containing easy-to-follow instructions. Follow the instructions to complete the tutorial, or press the Esc key to quit. (You might need to complete the on-screen instructions before you can quit the tutorial.)

IF YOU NEED HELP

To help you quickly resolve problems and to answer your questions, Windows provides online help that you can use from within Windows. Simply use one of the following techniques to open a window containing information:

- Choose a command from the Help menu on the menu bar.
- Press F1 while working within an application window.
- Choose the Help button in a dialog box.

The following list describes the commands provided by most applications' Help menu:

Command	Function
Contents	Opens a window showing the table of contents for topics concerning the selected application
Search for Help on	Opens a dialog box that allows you to type a subject name for which Windows displays a list of related help topics
How to Use Help	Opens a window showing explanatory text about Window's online help
About	Opens a window showing copyright information for the selected application

When you select a command from the Help menu or when you press F1, a window appears with help text and the following buttons (Figure 1-8). (Dimmed buttons are inappropriate for the current situation and cannot be selected.)

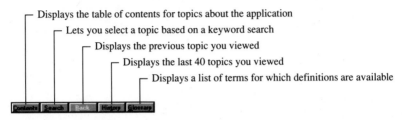

FIGURE 1-8. *The help buttons.*

Click on a help button to choose it.

Accessing Expanded Help

Additional information is available for terms or topics that are underlined in the help text. To obtain additional information, click on the underlined word.

Accessing Definitions

Definitions are available for terms that have a dotted underline in the help text. To see the definition of the term, click on the term.

If you encounter an unfamiliar term, you can look it up by opening the glossary window. To open the glossary window, click on the Glossary button. A glossary window similar to the one shown in Figure 1-9 appears.

FIGURE 1-9. *Help's glossary window.*

To view the definition of a specific term, follow these steps:

1. If necessary, drag the scroll box within the scroll bar to bring the term into view.

2. Click on the term.

Help displays the term's definition in a pop-up window similar to the one shown in Figure 1-10.

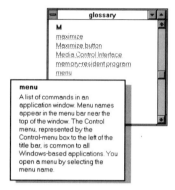

FIGURE 1-10. *A glossary definition in a pop-up window.*

To remove the pop-up window, click the mouse button or press any key. To close the glossary window, either double-click on the glossary window's Control-menu box or press Alt+F4.

Printing a Help Topic

To print the help topic, choose Print Topic from Help's File menu.

Choose Print Setup from Help's File menu if you want to select a printer other than the default printer, change the paper size or tray, change the print orientation (portrait or landscape), or change the print intensity for graphics. (You'll learn about these options in "Configuring a Printer" in Part III. Most users can simply use the default settings.)

Returning to Previous Help Topics

As you use Help to learn about various topics, there might be times when you want to return to a topic you were previously viewing. To do so, choose the Back button. Help displays the previous help topic. If you choose Back again, Help returns to the topic you viewed before the current one. You can view as many as 40 previous topics in this manner.

Help's History button also lets you quickly return to a previous topic. When you click on the History button, Help opens a History dialog box similar to Figure 1-11, which lists up to 40 previously viewed topics.

FIGURE 1-11. *The History dialog box.*

To return to a previous help topic, follow these steps:

1. If necessary, drag the scroll box until the topic becomes visible.

2. Double-click on the topic.

To close the History dialog box without making a selection, double-click on its Control-menu box or press Alt+F4.

Performing a Keyword Search

The Search button lets you search for help from a list of predefined keywords. When you click on the Search button, a dialog box appears, similar to Figure 1-12.

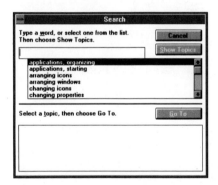

FIGURE 1-12. *The Search dialog box.*

The Search dialog box contains three fields: a text box near the top of the dialog box; a list box in the middle of the dialog box that contains all available keywords; and another list box at the bottom of the dialog box.

To search for a topic, follow these steps:

1. Select a keyword from the list box. (To quickly find the keyword, you can type the first letter or two of the desired keyword in the text box. The list box then moves to and highlights the first keyword that matches the letters you specified.)

2. If you find the keyword you desire, choose Go To. Help searches the help file for matching occurrences of the keyword and displays each match in the bottom list box.

3. If a reference in the bottom list box is of interest, double-click on the reference. Help will then display text about the topic.

Bookmarks

To help you learn efficiently as well as effectively, Windows provides a bookmark command that lets you mark your place in Help before you exit. Later—rather than browsing to find where you left off—you can return directly to the place you marked.

Defining a Bookmark

To define a bookmark, follow these steps:

1. Choose Define from Help's Bookmark menu. Windows displays the Bookmark Define dialog box, which contains the current help topic as the bookmark name (Figure 1-13).

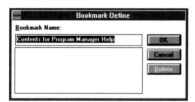

FIGURE 1-13. *The Bookmark Define dialog box.*

2. If you'd like, edit the name.

3. Choose OK to store the bookmark.

Accessing a Bookmark

To return to a marked position, follow these steps:

1. Open the Bookmark menu. A numbered list of every bookmark you've defined appears. (The list appears below the Define command.)

2. Click on the desired bookmark, or press the number key that corresponds to the desired bookmark.

Deleting a Bookmark

To delete a bookmark, follow these steps:

1. Open the Bookmark menu.

2. Choose the Define command.

3. Select the bookmark you want to delete.

4. Choose Delete.

5. Choose OK.

Annotations in Help Text

Help lets you *annotate* the help text. When you annotate help text, you place your own comments or reminders within the material.

Adding an annotation

To create a help annotation, follow these steps:

1. Choose Annotate from Help's Edit menu. Help opens the Annotate dialog box shown in Figure 1-14.

FIGURE 1-14. *Help's Annotate dialog box.*

2. Type in your own comments or reminders.

3. Choose Save.

After you annotate a topic, Help displays a paper clip in front of the topic's title, as shown in Figure 1-15.

FIGURE 1-15. *After you annotate a topic, it is displayed with a paper clip.*

To display a topic's annotated text, click on the paper clip.

Help displays the annotated text in a dialog box similar to the one in Figure 1-14. To close the dialog box, choose Cancel or press Alt+F4.

Removing an annotation

To remove an annotation, follow these steps:

1. Click on the paper clip. Help displays the annotated text in a dialog box.

2. Choose Delete.

Exiting Online Help

To exit online help, double-click on the Help window's Control-menu button or press Alt+F4.

EXITING WINDOWS

To exit Windows, follow these steps:

1. Close all open application windows, saving open files as necessary.

2. Choose Exit Windows from the Program Manager's File menu or double-click on the Program Manager's Control-menu box. The Exit Windows dialog box appears (Figure 1-16).

FIGURE 1-16. *The Exit Windows dialog box.*

3. Choose OK to exit.

PART II

Standard Applications

In this section, you'll learn about several key applications in Windows you use often: the Program Manager, the File Manager, Mail, Schedule+, the ClipBook Viewer, the Print Manager, the Task List, and the PIF Editor.

THE PROGRAM MANAGER

The central application of Windows is the *Program Manager*. The Program Manager is the window from which you start your applications. (See Figure 2-1.)

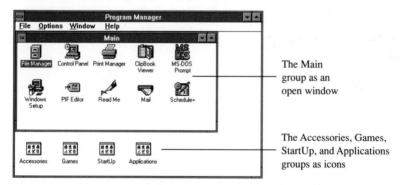

The Main
group as an
open window

The Accessories, Games,
StartUp, and Applications
groups as icons

FIGURE 2-1. *A group can appear as a window or as an icon.*

The Program Manager organizes applications into *groups*. A group can appear as an open window (called a *group window*) or as a minimized icon, as shown in Figure 2-1. A group window is a subwindow of the Program Manager window. Four groups—Main, Accessories, Games, and StartUp—are standard groups in Windows:

Group	Contents
Main	Applications that let you configure your hardware, customize the Windows environment, and make use of your network connections
Accessories	Applications that automate desktop tasks (Clock, Calculator, Notepad, and so on)

(continued)

continued

Group	Contents
Games	The games Solitaire and Minesweeper
StartUp	Programs you want to run each time Windows starts

You might also have one or more group windows containing applications for Windows and MS-DOS.

Adding a Program Group

To help you organize your work effectively, the Program Manager lets you create your own groups. For example, you might create a group called Business, which might contain a spreadsheet program, a word processor, and a project scheduler. To create a group, follow these steps:

1. Choose New from the Program Manager's File menu. The dialog box shown in Figure 2-2 appears.

FIGURE 2-2. *The New Program Object dialog box.*

2. Select Program Group, and choose OK. The dialog box shown in Figure 2-3 appears.

Temporarily Exiting Windows to Go to MS-DOS

If you need to leave Windows temporarily and go to MS-DOS, you can do so easily by choosing the MS-DOS Prompt icon from the Main group window. When you return to Windows, your previously open windows and files remain unchanged. To return to Windows from MS-DOS, use the Exit command as shown here:

```
C:\>EXIT
```

When you go to MS-DOS, do not turn off your computer without first returning to Windows and closing any applications that are running. This ensures that all files are saved correctly.

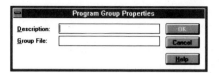

FIGURE 2-3. *The Program Group Properties dialog box.*

3. Type in the description you want to appear in this group window's title bar. Click on OK or press Enter.

Deleting a Program Group

If you decide a group is no longer necessary, you can delete it by following these steps:

1. Minimize and select the group you intend to delete. If you click on a group icon and its Control menu appears. Press Esc to close the Control menu.

2. Choose Delete from the File menu, or press the Delete key. A dialog box asking you to verify the deletion appears.

3. If the dialog box displays the correct group name, choose Yes; otherwise, choose No.

Adding an Application to a Group

After you create a group, you can add applications to it. To add an application to a group, follow these steps:

1. Select the desired group window or icon.

2. Choose New from the File menu. The New Program Object dialog box appears (Figure 2-2).

3. Select Program Item, and choose OK. The dialog box shown in Figure 2-4 appears.

FIGURE 2-4. *The Program Item Properties dialog box.*

4. Type the description that you want to appear beneath the application's icon. Do *not* press Enter.

5. Move to the Command Line text box. Type in the application's complete filename, including the drive letter, pathname, and filename extension. Do *not* press Enter.

6. Move to the Working Directory text box and type in the name of the directory where the application's data files are stored. Do *not* press Enter. You can leave this text box empty if the application has no data files or if the data files are stored in the same directory as the application.

7. Move to the Shortcut Key text box. A shortcut key is a combination of keys that, when pressed, makes the running application active. If you'd like to assign a shortcut key for this application, press a key. The Program Manager automatically creates the combination by adding the Ctrl and Alt keys to the key you pressed. You can create other combinations by pressing Ctrl, Shift, or both keys before pressing another key. Do *not* press Enter when you have finished.

8. If you'd like Windows to minimize the application when you run it, click on the Run Minimized check box, or press Alt+R.

9. Choose OK or press Enter to add the application to the group.

Deleting an Application from a Group

To delete an application from a group, follow these steps:

1. Select the icon of the application you want to delete.

2. Choose Delete from the File menu, or press the Delete key. A dialog box asking you to verify the deletion appears.

3. If the item specified is the application you want to delete, choose Yes; otherwise, choose No.

Moving or Copying an Application from One Group to Another

To move an application from one group to another, drag the application's icon into the desired group window or atop the desired group's icon.

To copy an application from one group to another, hold down the Ctrl key and then drag the application's icon into the desired group window or atop the desired group's icon.

Using the StartUp Group

You might want to run one or more applications each time you start Windows. If you copy the application to the StartUp group, as described above, Windows runs the application each time you start Windows.

Changing a Group Name

To change the name of a group, follow these steps:

1. Minimize and then select the desired group's window. If you click on the group icon and its Control menu appears. Press Esc to close the Control menu.

2. Choose Properties from the File menu. A dialog box similar to the one shown in Figure 2-5 appears.

FIGURE 2-5. *The Program Group Properties dialog box.*

3. Type a new group name in the Description text box, and choose OK.

Changing an Application's Description

To change an application's description, follow these steps:

1. Select the application's icon.

2. Choose Properties from the File menu. A dialog box similar to the one shown in Figure 2-6 appears.

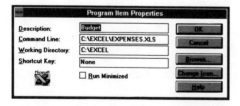

FIGURE 2-6. *The Program Item Properties dialog box.*

3. Type in the new description. Choose OK.

Tiling or Cascading Group Windows

The Program Manager's Window menu has two commands that help you view group windows. The first, Cascade, arranges group windows one on top of another, leaving the title bar of each window uncovered. The second, Tile, changes the size and position of each group window so that each is fully visible.

To arrange windows to best suit your needs, choose either Cascade or Tile from the Window menu.

Arranging Application and Group Icons

As you work with Windows, icons sometimes become disorganized within a group window. To tidy up the arrangement of icons, follow these steps:

1. Open the group window whose icons you want to arrange.

2. Choose Arrange Icons from the Window menu.

As you change the size of a group window, Windows might need to rearrange the icons so that you can view them. Choose Auto Arrange from the Options menu to have Windows automatically rearrange a resized group window's icons.

THE FILE MANAGER

The File Manager is a powerful application that lets you copy, delete, print, and rename files; run applications; and even perform disk operations such as formatting a new floppy disk. In addition, the File Manager lets you connect to network drives and share directories with other users on your network.

The File Manager Screen

When you start the File Manager, a screen similar to the one in Figure 2-7 on page 24 appears.

■ The *drive selector list* is a drop-down list you can use to quickly select a specific disk drive.

■ The *toolbar* is a set of buttons that correspond to common File Manager operations. You can determine which buttons appear on the toolbar by customizing it. (See ''Customizing the Toolbar'' later in Part II.) The following buttons are displayed by default:

Button	Action
	Connect to a network drive
	Disconnect from a network drive
	Share a directory
	Stop sharing a directory
	Display filenames and extensions only
	Display file details (name, size, date, time, and file attributes)
	Display files sorted alphabetically by name
	Display files sorted alphabetically by extension
	Display files sorted by size, from largest to smallest
	Display files sorted by date, from oldest to newest
	Send a message via Mail with the selected files attached

■ *Disk drive icons* represent the drives available to the File Manager. Drives can be of the following types: floppy disk drive, hard disk drive, network drive, RAM disk drive, and CD-ROM drive. Figure 2-7 shows the different disk drive icons.

■ The *directory path and file specification* show the full pathname of the current directory as well as the specification for the files shown.

■ The *disk volume label* is an optional name you can assign to a disk. (If your hard disk is unnamed, this field does not appear.)

■ The *directory tree* displays directories of the current drive. The File Manager lets you display all levels, specific levels, or one level of subdirectories in the directory tree. The File Manager displays directories using file folder icons. The File Manager displays the current directory's icon as an open folder.

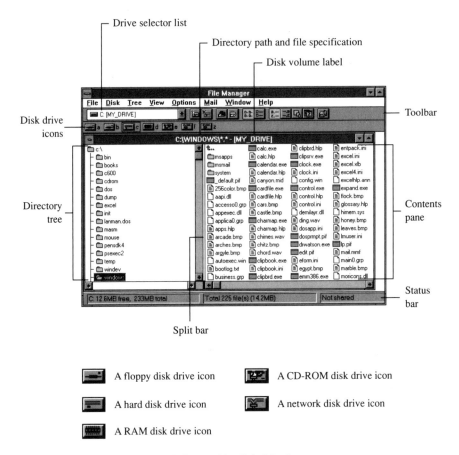

FIGURE 2-7. *The File Manager window and its disk drive icons.*

■ The *current directory* is the directory whose files the File Manager is currently displaying. The File Manager indicates the current directory by displaying an open file folder icon in the directory tree.

■ The *contents pane* shows the subdirectories and files in the current directory.

■ The *status bar* displays helpful information. It is split into three sections if an item in the directory tree or contents pane is selected. The contents of the first section depends on the type of item selected: If a directory in the directory tree is selected, it indicates the total number and available number of bytes on the current drive. If a file in the contents pane is selected, it indicates the file's size, date, and time. If multiple files or a directory is selected in the contents pane, it indicates the number of files selected and the total number of bytes consumed by the files. The second section displays the number of files in, and the disk space consumed by, the files in the current directory. The third section indicates whether the directory is shared. If you press the left mouse button when the pointer is over a button on the toolbar, the status bar displays a short description of the operation that will be performed when the mouse button is released.

Customizing the Toolbar

The File Manager lets you modify its toolbar. You can add buttons to it, remove buttons from it, and add or subtract space between buttons.

To modify the toolbar, double-click on the toolbar or choose Customize Toolbar from the Options menu. A dialog box similar to the one shown in Figure 2-8 appears.

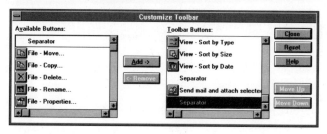

FIGURE 2-8. *The Customize Toolbar dialog box.*

The Toolbar Buttons list box displays the buttons that are currently on the toolbar in the order in which they appear. It also indicates—with the word *Separator*—the places where space is added between buttons. The Available Buttons list box displays the buttons that you can add to the toolbar. You can use the buttons, which correspond to commands available on File Manager's menus, to perform common operations:

Button   Action

    Move the selected file(s)

    Copy the selected file(s)

    Delete the selected file(s)

(continued)

continued

Button   Action

 Rename one or more files

 Assign file attributes to one or more selected files and view file information

 Print a file

 Create a directory

 Search a disk for one or more files

 Select files in the contents pane

 Select which file details to display in the contents pane

 Restrict the file types displayed in the contents pane

 Change the font, font style, or font size used by the File Manager

 Open a new window for the current directory

 Arrange directory windows so that they overlap, leaving each window's title bar uncovered

 Arrange directory windows horizontally, not overlapped

 Arrange directory windows vertically, not overlapped

 Display the contents of the File Manager's Help window

Adding a button or a separator to the toolbar

To add a button or a separator to the toolbar, follow these steps:

1. Select either the button you want to add or *Separator* from the Available Buttons list box.

2. Choose Add. The item you selected moves to the bottom of the Toolbar Buttons list box.

3. Position the item. The order of the items in the Toolbar Buttons list box dictates their order in the toolbar. Drag the added item in the list box to the place you want it.

NOTE: *You can also add a button or a separator to the toolbar by dragging the button or separator from the Available Buttons list box to the Toolbar Buttons list box and positioning it in the list before releasing the mouse button.*

Removing a button or a separator from the toolbar

To remove a button or a separator from the toolbar, select the button or Separator in the Toolbar Buttons list box and choose Remove. If you selected a button, the button moves from the Toolbar Buttons list box to the Available Buttons list box. A separator is simply deleted.

Positioning buttons and separators on the toolbar

To change the position of a button or a separator on the toolbar, select the item you want to move in the Toolbar Buttons list box. Then use the Move Up and Move Down buttons until the item is in the place you want it. You can also position an item by dragging it to the place you want it in the list.

Accepting your changes

When you finish modifying the toolbar, choose Close. The File Manager will immediately show the modified toolbar. If at any time you decide you don't like the changes, open the Customize Toolbar dialog box and choose Reset to return to the default toolbar display.

Changing Drives

You can change to any drive represented by a drive icon. To change to another drive, click on the drive's icon, select the drive from the drop-down drive selector list, or press Ctrl+X, where X is the letter of the drive you want to change to.

Changing Directories

To change to a different directory, click on the directory you want to move the *selection frame* (the dotted rectangle) to the desired directory.

Expanding and Collapsing Directories

MS-DOS lets you store files in *directories*. Directories are organizational tools that allow you to group related files. Think of a directory as a folder inside a filing cabinet.

Directories can also contain other directories. A directory that contains another directory is called a *parent directory*. A directory within another directory is called a *subdirectory*.

The File Manager's directory tree displays the directories on the current disk. Directories and subdirectories are displayed as icons that look like folders. (See Figure 2-7.) If a directory contains one or more subdirectories, its icon might contain a plus sign.

TIP: *If none of your directory icons contains a plus sign, choose Indicate Expandable Branches from the Tree menu.*

Expanding a parent directory

To expand a directory to reveal its subdirectories, double-click on the directory's icon. The File Manager expands the directory, showing its subdirectories and replacing the plus sign in the directory's icon with a minus sign.

To expand the directory to show all its subdirectories, including subdirectories within subdirectories, follow these steps:

1. Select the desired directory.
2. Choose Expand Branch from the Tree menu, or press the asterisk (∗) key.

Expanding the entire tree

To expand all directories on the current disk, choose Expand All from the Tree menu, or press Ctrl+∗. (In this case, you must use the asterisk key on the numeric keypad.)

Collapsing a directory

By *collapsing* a directory, you hide its subdirectories. To collapse an expanded directory, double-click on the directory's icon.

Viewing the Current Directory

The File Manager displays the current directory's files and subdirectories in the contents pane to the right of the directory tree. As you change directories, the File Manager updates the contents pane to display the files in the directory you've selected.

Each file in the contents pane has a corresponding icon that indicates the file type, as shown here:

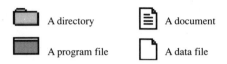

A directory   A document

A program file   A data file

Viewing Multiple Directories

Sometimes you might want to view the contents of two or more directories at the same time. To do so, open one or more additional directory windows. To open a directory window, choose New Window from the Window menu, or click on the toolbar's New Window button. The File Manager opens a second directory window, as shown in Figure 2-9.

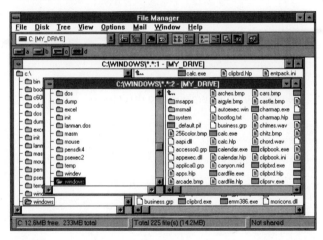

FIGURE 2-9. *The File Manager with two directory windows open.*

Within each directory window, you can change to any disk drive or directory. Additionally, the File Manager lets you move and copy files from one directory window to another.

TIP: *To open a new directory window for another drive, double-click on the drive's icon.*

Controlling the Display of Directory Windows

If you open multiple directory windows, you can move and size the windows as your needs require. The File Manager's Window menu has three commands that help you view directory windows. The first, Cascade, arranges directory windows one on top of another, leaving the title bar of each window uncovered. The second, Tile Horizontally, changes the size and position of each directory window so that each is fully visible and positions one above the other. The third, Tile Vertically, does nearly the same as Tile Horizontally, except that it positions the windows side by side.

To arrange windows to best suit your needs, choose one of these commands from the Window menu.

Closing a Directory Window

To close a directory window, double-click on the window's Control-menu box or press Ctrl+F4.

Sometimes, rather than closing a directory window, you might want to temporarily minimize the window to an icon. Click on the minimize button in the upper right corner of the window. When you do so, the directory window's icon appears at the bottom of the File Manager window. To expand the icon, double-click on it.

Running Applications

When you open a directory window, the File Manager displays the files the directory contains in the contents pane. You can run applications and work with files listed in the contents pane.

The File Manager provides a couple of ways to start an application.

■ If the application's name appears in the contents pane, you can double-click on the application's icon.

■ If the application's name does not appear, follow these steps:

1. Choose Run from the File menu. A dialog box similar to the one in Figure 2-10 appears.

FIGURE 2-10. *The Run dialog box.*

2. Type in the path and name of the application you want to run, along with any parameters the application requires.

3. Select the Run Minimized check box if you want the application to run in the background as an icon. Choose OK.

Changing Views

By default, a directory window contains a directory tree and a contents pane. The File Manager's View menu has commands that let you display only the directory tree, only the contents pane, or both (the default), as described here.

Command	Function
Tree and Directory	Displays the directory tree and the contents pane
Tree Only	Displays only the directory tree
Directory Only	Displays only the contents pane

By default, the Program Manager divides a directory window into two panes. The left pane of the window is the directory tree, and the right pane is the contents pane. The File Manager lets you move the split bar that divides the window, increasing the size of one pane while decreasing the size of the other. To change the divisions in a directory window, drag the split bar to the left or to the right.

Changing the File Information Displayed

By default, the File Manager displays only filenames and extensions in the contents pane. You can display other file characteristics by choosing commands from the View menu or by clicking on buttons in the toolbar.

Seeing file details

To display each file's name, extension, size, date and time stamp, and file attributes, choose All File Details from the View menu or click on the toolbar's File Details button. To hide these details, choose Name from the View menu or click on the toolbar's File Names And Extensions Only button.

Customizing contents pane information

To have specific file information appear in the contents pane, follow these steps:

1. Choose Partial Details from the View menu. A dialog box similar to the one in Figure 2-11 appears.

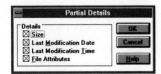

FIGURE 2-11. *The Partial Details dialog box.*

2. Select the file details you want the File Manager to display, or deselect the file details you don't want displayed.

3. Choose OK.

Changing the order of items in the contents pane

Within a contents pane, a list of directories followed by a list of file-names appears. Both the directory list and the filename list are sorted in alphabetic order. You can sort the files by name (filename), type (extension), size, or date either by choosing the appropriate command from the View menu or by clicking on a button in the File Manager's toolbar. The toolbar contains four buttons for sorting the directory contents: Sort By Name, Sort By Extension, Sort By Size, and Sort By Date.

Restricting the file types displayed

By default, a directory window displays the name of every type of file in the directory. To restrict which file types appear, follow these steps:

1. Choose By File Type from the View menu. A dialog box similar to the one in Figure 2-12 appears.

FIGURE 2-12. *The By File Type dialog box.*

2. Type in the wildcard pattern that corresponds to the files you want to display.

3. Select the check boxes of the file types you want to display, or deselect the file types you don't want to display.

4. Press Enter or choose OK.

Selecting Multiple Files

When you need to select more than one file, you can use one of several methods, depending on how the files are arranged in the contents pane.

Selecting consecutive files

To select files whose names appear consecutively in the contents pane, click on the first filename in the group. Then hold down the Shift key and click on the last filename in the group.

Selecting nonconsecutive files

To select multiple files whose names are not consecutive, hold down the Ctrl key and click on each filename you want.

Selecting all files

To select all the files in the contents pane, click on a file in the contents pane, and then press Ctrl+Slash(/).

Selecting or deselecting files by pattern

To select files that match a pattern, follow these steps:

1. Choose Select Files from the File menu. A dialog box similar to the one shown in Figure 2-13 appears.

FIGURE 2-13. *The Select Files dialog box.*

2. Type in the wildcard pattern that corresponds to the files you want to select or deselect. (For more information about pattern matching, see your MS-DOS manual.)

3. To select the files that match your pattern, choose the Select button. To deselect the files that match your pattern, choose the Deselect button.

Canceling selections

To cancel a selection, hold down the Ctrl key and click on the file.

To cancel all file selections, click on a file in the contents pane, or press Ctrl+Backslash(\).

Using the File Menu

The File Manager's File menu performs a variety of tasks, such as renaming and copying files. Figure 2-14 briefly describes each File command.

Command	Function
Open	Runs the selected application, or runs the application that created the selected document and loads the document into the application

FIGURE 2-14. *File menu commands.*   (continued)

Figure 2-14. *continued*

Command	Function
Move	Moves one or more files to a different disk or directory
Copy	Copies one or more files to a different disk or directory
Delete	Deletes one or more files or directories
Rename	Renames one or more files or a directory
Properties	Assigns new file attributes to one or more selected files
Run	Runs an application
Print	Prints a file
Associate	Associates a file type (extension) with an application
Create Directory	Creates a directory
Search	Searches a disk for one or more files
Select Files	Selects files in the contents pane
Exit	Exits the File Manager

Moving files and directories

To move files and directories, follow these steps:

1. Open a directory window that displays the files and directories you want to move. Open a directory window that displays the directory to which you want to move the files and directories. Make a portion of both windows visible.

2. Select the files and directories you want to move.

3. Drag the files and directories into the new directory window.

4. If the File Manager displays a dialog box asking you to confirm the move, choose Yes.

You can also move files and directories by choosing Move from the File menu, filling in the text boxes in the dialog box that appears, and choosing OK.

Copying files and directories

To copy files and directories, follow these steps:

1. Open a directory window that displays the files and directories you want to copy. Open a second directory window that displays the directory to which you want to copy the files and directories. Make a portion of both windows visible.

2. Select the files and directories to copy.

3. Hold down the Ctrl key and drag the selected files and directories into the new window.

4. If the File Manager displays a dialog box asking you to confirm the copy, choose Yes.

You can also copy files and directories by choosing Copy from the File menu, filling in the text boxes in the dialog box that appears, and choosing OK.

Deleting a file or directory

The File Manager lets you delete both files and directories. Note that when you delete a directory, all files and subdirectories in that directory are also deleted.

To delete a file or directory, follow these steps:

1. Select the file or directory you want to delete.

2. Choose Delete from the File menu or press the Delete key. A dialog box similar to the one shown in Figure 2-15 appears.

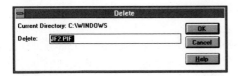

FIGURE 2-15. *The Delete dialog box.*

3. Choose OK.

4. If the File Manager displays a dialog box asking you to confirm the deletion, choose Yes.

Adding an item to a group window

The File Manager offers a convenient way to add an application or a document to a group window in the Program Manager. Simply drag the desired icon from the File Manager into the group window where you want to add the application or document.

Renaming a file or directory

To rename a file or directory, follow these steps:

1. Select the file or directory to rename.

2. Choose Rename from the File menu. A dialog box similar to the one shown in Figure 2-16 on the following page appears.

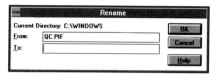

FIGURE 2-16. *The Rename dialog box.*

3. Type in the new name. Choose OK.

Assigning file attributes

The File Manager lets you assign new file attributes to one or more files. The following list describes the available attributes:

File Attribute	Meaning
Read Only	Prevents the file from being changed or deleted
Archive	Identifies the file as needing to be backed up
Hidden	Prevents the file from appearing in an MS-DOS directory list
System	Identifies a special MS-DOS system file

To assign file attributes to one or more files, follow these steps:

1. Select the desired files.

2. Choose Properties from the File menu. A dialog box similar to the one shown in Figure 2-17 appears.

3. Select the check boxes to assign the associated attributes, or deselect the check boxes to remove the associated attributes. Choose OK.

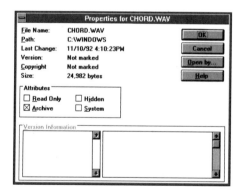

FIGURE 2-17. *The Properties dialog box.*

Note that you can choose Open By in the dialog box shown in Figure 2-17 to see who in your workgroup has the file open.

Printing a file

To print a file, follow these steps:

1. Select the file you want to print.

2. Choose Print from the File menu. A dialog box similar to the one in Figure 2-18 appears.

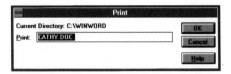

FIGURE 2-18. *The Print dialog box.*

3. Choose OK.

TIP: *If the Print Manager is running, a quick way to print a file is to drag the file's icon from the File Manager window to the Print Manager icon.*

NOTE: *A document must be associated with an application before it can be printed from the File Manager.*

Associating files

Every document file created with a Windows-based application has a *filename extension*. (For example, every Write document file has the WRI filename extension.) This extension—the characters at the end of the filename—can be *associated* with an application.

By associating an extension with an application, you can have Windows run the associated application—and load the selected file—each time you choose a file with that file extension. (For example, by simply double-clicking on any file with the WRI extension, you'd trigger Write to begin and load the file you chose.)

To associate a filename extension with an application, follow these steps:

1. Select a file with the desired filename extension from a directory window.

2. Choose Associate from the File menu. A dialog box similar to the one shown in Figure 2-19 appears.

FIGURE 2-19. *The Associate dialog box.*

3. If the application you want is in the Associate With list box, select the application.

4. If the Associate With list box does not contain the application you want, choose Browse. A dialog box similar to the one shown in Figure 2-20 appears.

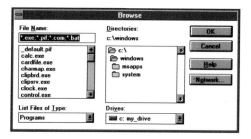

FIGURE 2-20. *The Browse dialog box.*

5. Choose the application's drive in the Drives drop-down list box, and the application's directory in the Directories list box. (Choose Network to connect to a new network drive.) Select the application's name in the File Name list box.

6. Choose OK. The Browse dialog box closes, and the appropriate information is added to the Associate dialog box. Choose OK.

Searching your disk for a file

You can use the File Manager to search for a file or type of file. The File Manager opens a window containing the path of the file or a list of the paths of the files matching the type you specified.

To search for a file, follow these steps:

1. Choose Search from the File menu. A dialog box similar to the one shown in Figure 2-21 appears.

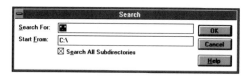

FIGURE 2-21. *The Search dialog box.*

2. Type the name of the file (or the pattern for the type of file) you want to search for in the Search For text box.

3. Type the name of the directory or path you want the File Manager to search in the Start From text box.

4. Select the Search All Subdirectories check box if you want the File Manager to search the subdirectories of the specified directory. Otherwise, the File Manager searches only the specified directory. Choose OK. If the File Manager locates one or more matching files, it opens a window listing the files, as shown in Figure 2-22.

FIGURE 2-22. *The Search Results window.*

Using the Disk Menu

The File Manager's Disk menu lets you copy, label, and format disks, as well as connect to network drives and manage shared directories. The following list describes the commands available on the Disk menu.

Command	Function
Copy Disk	Copies the contents of one floppy disk to another
Label Disk	Assigns a volume label to a disk
Format Disk	Formats a floppy disk
Make System Disk	Makes a disk a bootable disk
Connect Network Drive	Connects to a shared directory on a remote machine
Disconnect Network Drive	Disconnects from a shared directory on a remote machine
Share As	Allows a local directory to be shared by one or more users in your workgroup
Stop Sharing	Removes remote access to a local directory
Select Drive	Changes the currently selected drive to another drive

Copying one floppy disk to another

The File Manager lets you copy the contents of one floppy disk to a second floppy disk of identical size and capacity. The disk copy operation overwrites the contents of the second disk. If the second floppy disk is not formatted, the File Manager formats it for you.

Depending on whether your system contains one or two floppy disk drives, the steps you must perform to copy one floppy disk (called the *source disk*) to another floppy disk (called the *destination disk*) will differ. To perform a disk copy on a system with two floppy disk drives, follow these steps:

1. Insert the source disk into a disk drive. If you have dual disk drives of the same size and capacity, insert the destination disk into the second disk drive.

2. Choose Copy Disk from the Disk menu. The dialog box shown in Figure 2-23 appears.

FIGURE 2-23. *The Copy Disk dialog box.*

3. Choose the drive letter of the source disk from the Source In drop-down list.

4. Choose the drive letter of the destination disk from the Destination In drop-down list. (On systems whose two disk drives are of different size or capacity, specify the same drive for the source and destination drives.) Choose OK.

5. A dialog box appears, asking you to confirm the copy operation. Choose Yes and follow the instructions that appear.

To perform a single-drive disk copy operation, follow these steps:

1. Insert the source disk into the drive.

2. Choose Copy Disk from the Disk menu.

3. The File Manager will display a dialog box asking you to verify the copy operation. Choose Yes.

4. When the File Manager prompts you to insert the source or destination disk into the drive, do so and choose OK.

Labeling a disk

A volume label is a name of up to 11 characters you can assign to a disk to improve your disk organization. To assign a volume label to a disk, follow these steps:

1. Select the drive containing the disk you want to label.

2. Choose Label Disk from the Disk menu. A dialog box with a text box for the label appears. The text box contains the existing volume label if the disk has one.

3. Type in the volume label name you want, and choose OK.

Formatting a floppy disk

To format a floppy disk with the File Manager, follow these steps:

1. Insert the floppy disk into a drive.

2. Choose Format Disk from the Disk menu. A dialog box similar to the one shown in Figure 2-24 appears.

FIGURE 2-24. *The Format Disk dialog box.*

3. If necessary, select the drive the disk resides in from the Disk In drop-down list.

4. If necessary, select the disk's size in the Capacity drop-down list.

5. If you want to assign a volume label to the disk, select the Label text box and type in a volume name that has 11 or fewer characters.

6. If you want the disk to be bootable, select the Make System Disk check box.

7. If you want to reformat a previously formatted disk, select the Quick Format check box. A quick format creates a new file allocation table and root directory, but the disk is not scanned for bad areas. A quick format is much faster than a normal format, but use this option only on disks that you know to have no errors.

8. Choose OK.

9. If the File Manager displays a dialog box asking you to confirm the format operation, choose Yes.

Creating a system disk

Before you can boot MS-DOS from a floppy disk, the disk must contain special system files. To copy the system files to a floppy disk, use the following steps.

1. Choose Make System Disk from the Disk menu. A dialog box similar to the one shown in Figure 2-25 appears.

FIGURE 2-25. *The Make System Disk dialog box.*

2. Choose the drive containing the disk to which you want to copy the system files.

3. Choose OK.

Connecting to a network drive

A network drive is a shared drive or directory on another computer that is connected to the network. To connect to a network drive, follow these steps:

1. Click on the toolbar's Connect To Network Drive button. The File Manager will display a Connect Network Drive dialog box similar to the one shown in Figure 2-26.

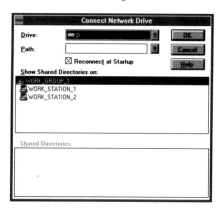

FIGURE 2-26. *The Connect Network Drive dialog box.*

2. Select a drive letter for the network drive from the Drive drop-down list. (The default letter is the next available one.)

3. Specify the network drive to which you want to connect. First select the remote computer from the Show Shared Directories On list box. (The list box displays both workgroup names and the computers in the workgroups.) Then select the directory (the network drive) to

which you want to connect from the Shared Directories list box. If you want to connect to a drive you had connected to previously, select the drive's path from the Path drop-down list.

4. Choose OK.

5. If the directory is password protected, a dialog box prompting for the password will appear. Type in the appropriate password and choose OK.

The File Manager will add a disk drive icon to its window and open a directory window for the network drive.

Disconnecting from a network drive

When you no longer need access to a network drive, disconnect the drive as follows:

1. Click on the toolbar's Disconnect Network Drive button. The File Manager displays a Disconnect Drive dialog box similar to the one shown in Figure 2-27.

FIGURE 2-27. *The Disconnect Drive dialog box.*

2. Select the drive from which you want to disconnect from the Drive list box.

3. Choose OK.

Sharing a directory

A shared directory is a directory that is accessible both to the user at the computer that contains it and to other users in the workgroup. To share a directory with other users, follow these steps:

1. Select the directory to share, and click on the toolbar's Share Directory button. The File Manager displays a Share Directory dialog box similar to the one shown in Figure 2-28 on the following page.

2. In the Share Name text box, type a meaningful name by which users will refer to this directory, or use the directory name that Windows provides as the default.

3. If the directory specified in the Path text box is not the directory you want to share, type in the correct directory path.

FIGURE 2-28. *The Share Directory dialog box.*

4. Optionally, you can type in a description of the directory's use in the Comment text box. The comment will be shown in the Shared Directories list box of the Connect Network Drive dialog box to help users determine which shared directory to choose.

5. If you want the directory shared each time Windows starts, select the Re-share At Startup check box.

6. Select the access type that controls what users in your workgroup can do with the files they find in your shared directory:

Access Type	Function
Read-Only	Users cannot delete, create, or modify files.
Full	Users can control files as if the directory were local to their computers, creating, changing, or deleting files.
Depends On Password	User access depends on the password entered.

7. If you choose Read-Only or Full and you want to protect the directory with a password, type in a password. If you choose Depends On Password, specify two passwords: one that allows read-only access and another that allows full access.

8. Choose OK.

Stop sharing a directory

If users in your workgroup no longer require access to a directory, remove the shared access by following these steps:

1. Click on the toolbar's Stop Sharing Directory button. The File Manager displays a Stop Sharing Directory dialog box similar to the one shown in Figure 2-29.

2. Select the directory that you want to stop sharing.

3. Choose OK.

FIGURE 2-29. *The Stop Sharing Directory dialog box.*

Determining the Amount of Available Memory

To determine the amount of available memory on your system, choose About from the Help menu. A dialog box similar to the one shown in Figure 2-30 appears, displaying information about Windows and the amount of available memory.

FIGURE 2-30. *The About File Manager dialog box.*

Controlling Confirmation Dialog Boxes

By default, the File Manager displays dialog boxes confirming several operations, such as replacement and deletion of files. You can control whether these confirmation dialog boxes appear by using the Confirmation command from the Options menu. The following list describes the available confirmations:

Confirmation	Meaning
File Delete	A warning before files are deleted
Directory Delete	A warning before a subdirectory is deleted
File Replace	A warning before an existing file is overwritten
Mouse Action	A warning before files dragged by a mouse are copied or moved
Disk Commands	A warning before a disk is formatted or copied

To enable or disable one or more confirmations, follow these steps:

1. Choose Confirmation from the Options menu. A dialog box similar to the one shown in Figure 2-31 appears.

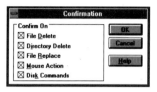

FIGURE 2-31. *The Confirmation dialog box.*

2. Select a check box to enable confirmation of an operation. Deselect the check box to turn off confirmation. Choose OK when you're satisfied with the confirmation settings.

Selecting a File Manager Font

The File Manager lets you select the font used to display file and directory names. To select a font, follow these steps:

1. Choose Font from the Options menu. A dialog box similar to the one shown in Figure 2-32 appears.

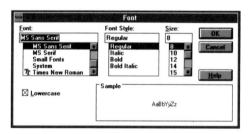

FIGURE 2-32. *The Font dialog box.*

2. Select a font from the Font list box. The Sample box shows several characters drawn in the font you've selected.

3. Select a font style from the Font Style list box. The Sample box shows several characters drawn in the font style you've selected.

4. Select a font size from the Size list box. The Sample box shows several characters drawn in the font size you've selected.

5. If you prefer to see file and directory names in lowercase characters, select the Lowercase check box; otherwise, deselect the Lowercase check box.

6. Choose OK.

Other File Manager Options

By using the Options menu, you can customize the File Manager to your liking, as described in the following list. A check mark in front of a command on the menu means that the command is active.

Command	Function
Toolbar	Controls whether the toolbar appears in the File Manager window
Drivebar	Controls whether the available disk drive icons appear in the File Manager window
Status Bar	Controls whether the status bar appears at the bottom of the File Manager window
Open New Window on Connect	Controls whether the File Manager opens a new window when you connect to a network drive
Minimize on Use	Controls whether the File Manager is minimized when you start another application from the File Manager
Save Settings on Exit	Saves the positions of open directory windows when you exit the File Manager

Exiting the File Manager

To exit the File Manager, double-click on the File Manager's Control-menu box, or choose Exit from the File menu.

MAIL

Mail allows users connected to a network to exchange information (messages) electronically. To use Mail, you must connect to your workgroup's postoffice. The postoffice, which is contained in a shared directory, manages the messages exchanged between users and maintains a list of members of the postoffice. A user can send messages to and receive messages from those users who are members of the same postoffice.

Setting Up Mail

To use Mail, you must first make a network connection to your workgroup's postoffice. The first time you double-click on the Mail icon to run Mail, the dialog box shown in Figure 2-33 on the following page appears.

FIGURE 2-33. *The Welcome To Mail dialog box.*

If your workgroup has a postoffice, connect to it. If it doesn't have a post-office, and if you want to set up one on your computer, create a new postoffice.

Connecting to a postoffice

To connect to a postoffice, follow these steps:

1. Select the Connect To A Remote Postoffice option button in the Welcome To Mail dialog box.

2. Choose OK. The dialog box shown in Figure 2-34 appears.

FIGURE 2-34. *The Network Disk Resources dialog box.*

3. Specify the network path of the postoffice to which you want to con-nect. First select the remote computer that contains the postoffice from the Show Shared Directories On list box. (The list box displays both workgroup names and the computers in the workgroups.) Then select the directory of the postoffice from the Shared Directories list box.

4. Choose OK.

5. If the postoffice is password protected, a dialog box prompting you for the password will appear. Type in the appropriate password and choose OK. Mail then displays the dialog box shown in Figure 2-35.

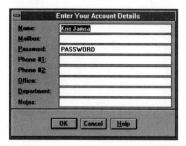

FIGURE 2-35. *The Enter Your Account Details dialog box.*

6. Type the information requested in the dialog box. You must fill in the first three fields. Your name is the name that others use to identify you when sending you messages. You use your mailbox name and password when you sign into Mail. Optionally, fill in the remaining fields. This information will be available to all the users in your postoffice.

7. Choose OK. Mail displays your mail folders and the messages contained in the current folder, as shown in Figure 2-38 on page 51.

Creating a new postoffice

If your workgroup doesn't have a postoffice and if you want to create and maintain the workgroup's postoffice on your computer, follow these steps:

1. Select the Create A New Workgroup Postoffice option button in the Welcome To Mail dialog box. Mail displays a message asking you to confirm that you want to create and administer a new postoffice.

2. Choose Yes. A dialog box similar to the one shown in Figure 2-36 appears.

FIGURE 2-36. *The Create Workgroup Postoffice dialog box.*

3. Select the drive and directory that will contain the postoffice.

4. Choose OK. Mail then displays the dialog box shown earlier, in Figure 2-35.

5. Type the information requested in the dialog box. You must fill in the first three fields. The name you enter is the name that others use to identify you when sending you messages. You use the mailbox name and password when you sign into Mail. Optionally, fill in the remaining fields. This information will be available to all the users in your postoffice.

7. Choose OK. Mail displays a dialog box letting you know that the postoffice was created and telling you that you must share the directory that contains the postoffice.

8. Choose OK. Mail displays your mail folders and the messages contained in the current folder, as shown in Figure 2-38.

9. Open the File Manager and share the directory. Be sure to allow full access. Optionally, specify a password.

Signing In

When you start Mail, Mail displays the Mail Sign In dialog box, which prompts you for your mailbox name and password, as shown in Figure 2-37.

FIGURE 2-37. *The Mail Sign In dialog box.*

Type in the mailbox name and password you chose when you set up Mail and choose OK. After you successfully sign in, Mail displays your mail folders and the list of messages contained in the current folder, as shown in Figure 2-38.

The following list describes the four default folders provided by Mail:

Folder	Function
Deleted Mail	Contains messages you have discarded. By default, the messages in this folder are discarded when you exit Mail. (You can keep the messages in the Deleted Mail folder by choosing Options from the Mail menu and deselecting the Empty Deleted Mail Folder When Exiting check box.)
Inbox	Contains messages sent to you by other users
Sent Mail	Contains copies of messages you have sent to other users
Outbox	Holds the messages you have sent to other users until Mail communicates with the postoffice. Any waiting messages are then taken from the folder and sent to the recipients.

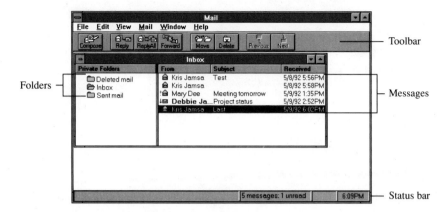

FIGURE 2-38. *The Mail window.*

Changing Your Mail Password

For security purposes, you should periodically change your Mail password. To change your password, follow these steps:

1. Choose Change Password from the Mail menu. Mail displays the Change Password dialog box, shown in Figure 2-39.

FIGURE 2-39. *The Change Password dialog box.*

2. Type your current password in the Old Password text box.

3. Type your new password in the New Password text box.

4. Repeat the new password in the Verify New Password text box.

5. Choose OK.

Sending a Message

You can use Mail to send a message to one or more users in your postoffice. To send a message, follow these steps:

1. Click on the toolbar's Compose button. Mail displays the Send Note form, as shown in Figure 2-40 on the following page.

2. In the To field, type the names of the users to whom you want to send the message. If you type multiple names, separate the names with semicolons. If you're not certain of the name of the user, click on

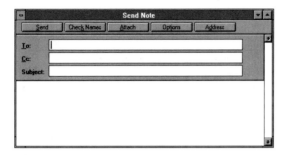

FIGURE 2-40. *The Send Note form.*

the Address button to display a directory of users. See the section titled "Using Address Books" for more information about the directory.

3. If you want to send a "courtesy copy" of the message, type the names of the users to whom you want to send a copy in the Cc field. If you type multiple names, separate the names with semicolons.

4. Type a brief description of the message's subject in the Subject field.

5. Type the text of your message in the area below the Subject field. When you are done, click on the Send button to send the message.

Mail places the message in the Outbox and sends it to the recipients the next time it communicates with the postoffice.

Editing message text

In addition to the standard keyboard editing keys, Mail offers commands that make editing your messages simple. The following list describes Mail's Edit menu commands:

Command	Action
Undo	Reverses the previous edit
Cut	Cuts the selected text to the Clipboard
Copy	Copies the selected text to the Clipboard
Paste	Inserts text from the Clipboard
Paste Special	Embeds an object from the Clipboard in a message
Delete	Erases the selected text
Select All	Selects the contents of the entire message
Object	Edits an attached file or an embedded object
Insert Object	Creates and embeds an object
Insert From File	Inserts the contents of a text file into a message

Attaching a file to a message

To attach a file to a message, follow these steps:

1. Position the insertion point where you want the attached file's icon to appear in your message.

2. Click on the Attach button. The Attach dialog box appears, as shown in Figure 2-41.

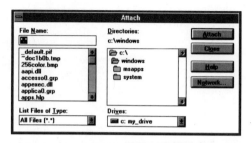

FIGURE 2-41. *The Attach dialog box.*

3. Select the file you want to attach. (Choose Network to connect to a new network drive.)

4. Choose Close. Mail attaches the file and places the file's icon in the message.

Embedding an object in a message

Mail enables you to take advantage of the object linking and embedding (OLE) capabilities of Windows by embedding objects in messages. An embedded object maintains a link to the application in which it was created. Mail offers two commands for embedding objects in messages: Paste Special and Insert Object. Paste Special inserts objects that have already been created. Insert Object prompts you to create an object and then inserts it.

To embed an object using the Paste Special command, follow these steps:

1. Open an application (such as Paintbrush) that can create objects.

2. Select the information that you want as your object and copy it to the Clipboard.

3. Return to Mail and position the insertion point where you want the object to appear in your message.

4. Choose Paste Special from the Edit menu. A dialog box similar to the one shown in Figure 2-42 on the following page appears.

FIGURE 2-42. *The Paste Special dialog box.*

5. Select the correct object type from the Data Type list box.

6. Choose Paste. The embedded object in the message will look exactly the same as it does in its application.

To embed an object using the Insert Object command, follow these steps:

1. Position the insertion point where you want the object to appear in your message.

2. Choose Insert Object from the Edit menu. Mail displays the Insert Object dialog box, as shown in Figure 2-43.

FIGURE 2-43. *The Insert Object dialog box.*

3. Choose the type of object you want to create from the Object Type list box and choose OK. Windows opens the application corresponding to the object's type.

4. Create the object, and then choose the Exit command from the File menu.

5. Choose Yes in the dialog box that appears. Windows closes the application and embeds the object you created in the Mail message. The embedded object will look exactly the same as it does in its application.

Setting message options

Message options let you control a message's priority (which Mail conveys to the recipient with the icon it displays in the message list), whether you get a return receipt (which tells you the receiver has read the message), and whether Mail saves the messages you send. To set message options, follow these steps:

1. Select the Options button in the Send Note form. Mail displays the Options dialog box, as shown in Figure 2-44.

FIGURE 2-44. *The Options dialog box.*

2. Select the options you want.

3. Choose OK.

Receiving a Message

If the Mail window is open, or if it is minimized to an icon, when another user sends you a message, your system will beep and your cursor will momentarily change to the shape of an envelope, notifying you of the message. If Mail is not running, you will not be notified of the new message. To check and read your messages, perform these steps:

1. Sign into Mail.

2. If it isn't already open, open the Inbox folder by double-clicking on its icon. The list of messages contains both old and new messages. New or unread messages have a closed-envelope icon. Messages you have already read have an opened-envelope icon.

3. If you have a new message, double-click on it. Mail opens a message window, displaying the message contents.

4. You can click on the the Previous or the Next button to open the previous or the next message in the list without having to go back to the list itself.

5. When you're finished reading messages, close the message window by double-clicking on its Control-menu box.

Accessing an attached file

To open a file that was attached to a message sent to you, double-click on the file's icon in the message. To save an attached file, follow these steps:

1. Select the file's icon in the message.

2. Choose Save Attachment from the File menu. Mail displays a Save Attachment dialog box similar to the one in Figure 2-45.

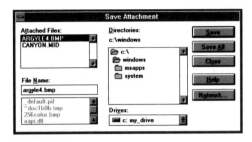

FIGURE 2-45. *The Save Attachment dialog box.*

3. Select the file you want to save from the Attached Files list box.

4. Optionally, you can change the drive, directory, and filename to which the file will be saved. (Choose Network to connect to a new network drive.)

5. Choose Save.

6. Choose Close when you're finished saving attachments.

Replying to a Message

To reply to only the sender of a message, follow these steps:

1. Display or select from the list the message to which you want to reply.

2. Click the toolbar's Reply button. Mail opens a new Send Note form with the name of the sender in the To field and a copy of the message to which you're replying.

3. Type your reply message.

4. Choose Send.

To reply to the sender and to everyone who received the message (everyone specified in the To and Cc fields), follow these steps:

1. Display or select from the list the message to which you want to reply.

2. Click on the toolbar's ReplyAll button. Mail opens a new Send Note form with the names of the sender and the recipients in the To and Cc fields and a copy of the message to which you're replying.

3. Type your reply message.

4. Choose Send.

Forwarding a Message

To forward a message to one or more users, follow these steps:

1. Display or select from the list the message you want to forward.

2. Click on the toolbar's Forward button. Mail opens a new Send Note form that contains a copy of the message you are forwarding.

3. In the To field, type the name or names of the individuals to whom you want to forward the message.

4. Modify the message text if desired.

5. Choose Send.

Printing a Message

To print one or more messages, follow these steps:

1. Select the message or messages you want to print.

2. Choose Print from the File menu. Mail displays the Print dialog box, shown in Figure 2-46.

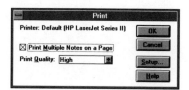

FIGURE 2-46. *The Print dialog box.*

3. If you are printing multiple messages and want each message on its own page, deselect the Print Multiple Notes On A Page check box.

4. Select the print quality you want in the Print Quality drop-down list.

5. Choose OK.

Saving a Message to a Text File

To save a message to a text file, follow these steps:

1. Display or select from the list the message you want to save.

2. Choose Save As from the File menu. Mail displays a Save Message dialog box.

3. Optionally, you can change the drive, directory, and filename to which the message will be saved. (Choose Network to connect to a new network drive.)

4. Choose OK.

Deleting Messages

To delete one or more messages, follow these steps:

1. Select the messages to delete.

2. Drag the messages to the Deleted Mail folder or click on the toolbar's Delete button.

If the Empty Deleted Mail Folder When Exiting check box in the Mail menu's Options dialog box is selected, the deleted messages will be discarded when you exit Mail. If the check box is not selected, discard the messages by selecting them in the Deleted Mail folder and clicking on the toolbar's Delete button.

Managing Mail Folders

Mail folders let you organize your messages. Not only can you create folders at the same level as Mail's default folders, but you can also create folders within folders, called *subfolders*.

Mail offers two types of folders: private folders and shared folders. Only you can access your private folders. Everyone in your postoffice can access the shared folders. By default, you view your private folders. To see the shared folders, click on the Private Folders button above the list of folders. The button is now labeled ''Shared Folders.'' Click on the button again to return to your private folders.

Mail provides several features that help you manage your folders.

Creating a folder

To create a folder, follow these steps:

1. Choose New Folder from the File menu. Mail displays the New Folder dialog box, shown in Figure 2-47.

FIGURE 2-47. *The New Folder dialog box.*

3. Type the folder name. Folder names can contain both uppercase and lowercase letters and can contain spaces.

4. Specify whether the folder will be private or shared.

5. Choose the Options button. Mail expands the New Folder dialog box, as shown in Figure 2-48.

FIGURE 2-48. *The expanded New Folder dialog box.*

6. For a top-level folder, select the Top Level Folder option button. For a subfolder, select the name of the folder within which you want the subfolder to reside.

7. If the folder will be shared, select any combination of the Read, Write, and Delete check boxes to specify the actions other users can perform on the folder and its contents.

8. Choose OK.

Deleting a folder

To delete a folder, follow these steps:

1. Select the folder you want to delete.

2. Drag the folder to the Deleted Mail folder or click on the toolbar's Delete button. Mail displays a dialog box warning you that all messages within the folder will also be deleted.

3. Choose Yes.

Moving messages

To move messages from one folder to another, follow these steps:

1. Select the messages you want to move.

2. Drag the messages to the destination folder, or select the messages and click on the toolbar's Move button. When you click on the Move button, Mail displays the Move Messages dialog box, shown in Figure 2-49 on the following page.

FIGURE 2-49. *The Move Messages dialog box.*

3. Select whether you want to move the messages to a private folder or a shared folder.

4. Select the destination folder from the list of folders. If you want to create a new folder to which you will move the messages, click on the New button. Mail displays the New Folder dialog box for you to fill in.

5. Choose OK.

Copying messages

To copy messages from one folder to another, follow these steps:

1. Select the messages you want to copy.

2. Hold down the Ctrl key and drag the messages to the destination folder, or select the messages and choose Copy from the File menu. When you choose the Copy command, Mail displays the Copy Messages dialog box, shown in Figure 2-50.

FIGURE 2-50. *The Copy Messages dialog box.*

3. Select whether you want to copy the messages to a private folder or to a shared folder.

4. Select the destination folder from the list of folders. If you want to create a new folder to which you will copy the messages, click on the New button. Mail displays the New Folder dialog box for you to fill in.

5. Choose OK.

Moving a folder

To move a folder, follow these steps:

1. Select the folder you want to move.

2. Drag the folder to the destination folder, or select the folder and click on the toolbar's Move button. When you click on the Move button, Mail displays the Move Folder dialog box, shown in Figure 2-51. Because you cannot move a folder between the private and the shared folder lists, the option buttons in the Type box are disabled.

FIGURE 2-51. *The Move Folder dialog box.*

3. Select the destination folder from the list of folders. If you want to create a new folder to which you will copy the folder, click on the New button. Mail displays the New Folder dialog box for you to fill in.

4. Choose OK.

Expanding and collapsing subfolder display

To collapse the display of subfolders, click on the minus sign that appears to the left of the folder name. To expand the display of subfolders, click on the plus sign that appears to the left of the folder name.

Retrieving deleted messages

When you delete a message, Mail places the message in the Deleted Mail folder. Unless you specify otherwise in the Mail menu's Options dialog box, the message is discarded when you exit Mail. Until that time, you can retrieve a deleted message by simply moving the message from the Deleted Mail folder.

Searching for a Specific Message

To search your Mail folders for a specific message, follow these steps:

1. Choose Message Finder from the File menu. Mail displays a Message Finder window as shown in Figure 2-52 on the following page.

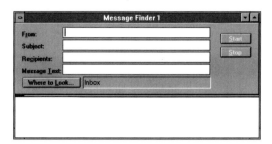

FIGURE 2-52. *The Message Finder window.*

2. Type in the information corresponding to the message for which you want to search.

3. Choose the Where To Look button. Mail displays a Where To Look dialog box similar to the one shown in Figure 2-53.

FIGURE 2-53. *The Where To Look dialog box.*

4. Select the folders you want to search, or select the Look In All Folders option button.

5. Choose OK.

6. Select the Unread Only check box if you want Mail to search only unread messages.

7. Choose Start. Mail searches for messages that match the information you specified and places the headings of the messages it finds in the bottom portion of the Message Finder window. You can open a message in the list by double-clicking on its heading.

If you leave the Message Finder window open, Mail will check all new messages that you receive and will add them to its list if they match the information you specified.

Backing Up the Message File

Mail stores your folders and messages in one file. To back up your message file, follow these steps:

1. Choose Backup from the Mail menu. Mail displays the Backup dialog box.

2. Type a filename in the File Name text box, and select the location where you want the backup file stored. (Choose Network to connect to a new network drive.)

3. Choose OK.

Restoring a Message File

If, when you start, Mail cannot locate your message file, Mail will display a dialog box asking you to choose a message file. To restore your backup file, follow these steps:

1. Locate and select the backup file.

2. When Mail asks if you want to convert the file, choose OK.

Selecting Mail Options

To customize Mail, follow these steps:

1. Choose Options from the Mail menu. Mail displays the Options dialog box, shown in Figure 2-54.

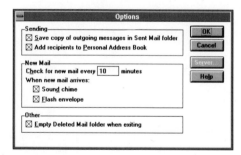

FIGURE 2-54. *The Options dialog box.*

2. Select the options you want.

3. Choose OK.

Using Address Books

To help you determine a user's electronic mail name (address), Mail provides an address book. To look up a user in the address book, choose Address Book from the Mail menu. Mail displays the Address Book dialog box, shown in Figure 2-55 on the following page. The address book displays a directory that lists the users in your postoffice.

Directory
Personal Address Book
Find
New Address

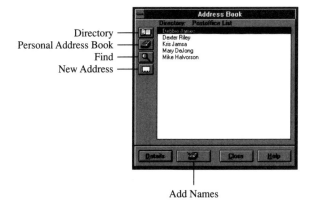

Add Names

FIGURE 2-55. *The Address Book dialog box.*

Because the number of users in the postoffice directory can be quite large, Mail lets you add names to a personal address book. Conceptually, you can view the postoffice directory as a phone book, and your personal address book as a personal card file.

Viewing your personal address book

To view your personal address book, follow these steps:

1. Choose Address Book from the Mail menu.

2. In the Address Book dialog box, click on the Personal Address Book button.

To return to the postoffice directory, click on the Directory button, select Postoffice List, and choose OK.

Using address book names

When you are composing a message, you can use the address book to select the names of people to whom you will send the message. To select names from the address book, follow these steps:

1. While composing a message, click on the Address button in the Send Note form. Mail displays the Address dialog box, as shown in Figure 2-56.

2. Drag the desired names into the To and Cc fields of the dialog box.

3. Choose OK. Mail inserts the names in the To and Cc fields of your message.

FIGURE 2-56. *The Address dialog box.*

Updating your personal address book

Mail lets you add names to and remove names from your personal address book. To add names, follow these steps:

1. Choose Address Book from the Mail menu.

2. Select the names desired from the postoffice directory.

3. Click on the Add Names button.

4. Choose the Close button.

To remove a name from your personal address book, follow these steps:

1. Choose Address Book from the Mail menu.

2. Open your personal address book.

3. Select the names you want to remove.

4. Choose the Remove button.

5. When Mail displays a dialog box to verify the removal, choose Yes.

Searching for a user name

There may be times when you are not sure of the spelling of a user's name. To search for a user's name, follow these steps:

1. Choose Address Book from the Mail menu.

2. Click on the Find button. Mail displays the Name Finder dialog box, shown in Figure 2-57.

FIGURE 2-57. *The Name Finder dialog box.*

3. Type in as much of the name as you know and choose Find.

If Mail does not find a match, it will display a dialog box stating so. Otherwise, Mail will display a list of all the users in the address book whose names begin with the letters you specified.

Creating a new address

To add the address of someone on a different electronic Mail system or in another postoffice, follow these steps:

1. Click on the New Address button.

2. Choose the type of entry you want to create and choose OK. Mail displays a New User dialog box that contains fields specific to the type of entry being created.

3. Enter the details of the address.

4. Choose the Add Names button.

Getting details about a user

Mail maintains detailed information, such as telephone and office number, about each user. Using this information, you can verify that a user's name corresponds to the person you're looking for, or you can find out how to reach the person by phone. To view details about a user, follow these steps:

1. Choose Address Book from the Mail menu.

2. Select the user's name.

3. Choose the Details button. Mail displays a dialog box containing information about the user.

4. If you selected the name from a list other than your personal address book, you can add the user to your personal address book by clicking on the Add Names button.

5. If you selected a name from your personal address book, choose Cancel. Otherwise, choose Close.

Personal Groups

Many times you will send the same set of messages to a group of people, such as your project team members. Mail lets you combine a set of user names into a named group called a *personal group*. When you later send a message to the group's name, everyone in the personal group will receive the message.

Creating a personal group

To create a personal group, follow these steps:

1. Choose Personal Groups from the Mail menu. Mail displays the Personal Groups dialog box, shown in Figure 2-58.

FIGURE 2-58. *The Personal Groups dialog box.*

2. Choose the New button. Mail displays the New Group dialog box, which prompts you to enter a name.

3. Type a meaningful group name and choose the Create button. Mail displays a dialog box for specifying the members of the group, as shown in Figure 2-59.

FIGURE 2-59. *A dialog box for specifying the members of a personal group.*

4. Select the names of the group members from the address book and drag them to the Group Members list.

5. Choose OK.

Removing a personal group

To remove a personal group when you no longer need it, follow these steps:

1. Choose Personal Groups from the Mail menu.

2. Select the name of the personal group you want to remove.

3. Choose the Remove button.

4. When Mail displays a dialog box asking you to verify the removal, choose Yes.

5. Choose Close.

Changing a personal group's members

To change the membership of a personal group, follow these steps:

1. Choose Personal Groups from the Mail menu.

2. Select the name of the group you want to edit.

3. Choose Edit. Mail displays the Personal Groups dialog box (Figure 2-59).

To remove a name, select the name in the Group Members list box and press the Delete key. To add a name to the list, select the name from the directory list and drag it to the Group Members list box.

Working Offline

If the server containing your Mail postoffice is not available, you can create messages offline. You can't send the message until you connect to the server. Instead, your message remains in the Outbox folder.

If you later try to access Mail and the server is unavailable, Mail will ask you if you want to work offline. If you do, choose Yes.

When you finish composing a message offline, choose the Send button as you would normally do. Mail will store the message in your Outbox folder. The next time you connect to the server, the messages in your Outbox folder will be sent automatically.

Managing the Workgroup Postoffice

If your workgroup's postoffice is on your computer, you are responsible for managing it. Mail adds the Postoffice Manager command to the Mail menu when it sets up the postoffice on your computer. When you choose this command, the dialog box shown in Figure 2-60 appears.

You can modify the information about any user in your postoffice by selecting the user's name and choosing the Details button. Make any changes you want in the dialog box that appears and choose OK.

To add a user to the postoffice, choose the New User button. Fill in at least the first three text boxes—Name, Mailbox, and Password—in the dialog box that appears and choose OK.

FIGURE 2-60. *The Postoffice Manager dialog box.*

To remove a user from the postoffice, select the user's name and choose Remove User. When Mail displays a dialog box asking you to verify the removal, choose Yes.

To view information about the postoffice's shared folders, choose the Shared Folders button. To compress the files, choose Compress in the dialog box that appears.

SCHEDULE+

Schedule+ is an application that helps you manage projects, track your daily tasks, and coordinate and schedule appointments with other users in your workgroup. Schedule+ makes it easy to schedule meetings—you can see at a glance when everyone is available. You can also allow other users, depending on the privileges you grant them, to view, schedule, or change your appointments. Schedule+ even lets you designate a specific individual to serve as your assistant and oversee your appointments. Schedule+ provides the ideal tool for handling your workgroup's scheduling headaches.

Starting Schedule+

Double-click on the Schedule+ icon to start the application. Because Schedule+ is tightly integrated with Mail, if you don't have Mail running when you start Schedule+, Schedule+ will display the Mail Sign In dialog box, shown previously in Figure 2-37.

Type in your Mail user name and your password. Schedule+ displays the Messages window and the main Schedule+ window, which displays your appointments, as shown in Figure 2-61 on the following page.

When you start Schedule+, the window displays the current day's appointments list. Schedule+ can also display a weekly planner and a list of tasks. Click on the tabs on the left side of the window to switch between the views.

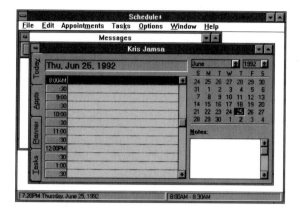

FIGURE 2-61. *The Schedule+ window.*

Viewing Appointments

By default, Schedule+ displays the current day's appointments in the appointments list. However, using the calendar that appears on the right side of the window, you can select any day in the range January 1, 1920, through December 31, 2019.

Selecting a day within the current month

To select a day within the current month, click on the corresponding date within the calendar. Schedule+ displays the day's appointments. Note that the status bar continues to display the current date and time. The calendar indicates the current day by displaying it in a box.

Selecting a day outside the current month

To display the appointments for a day whose date is not in the month that is currently displayed, use the calendar's month and year drop-down lists to select the month and year. Then click on the day you want.

Selecting a specific date

In addition to letting you select a specific date using the calendar, Schedule+ lets you quickly type in or select a date using the Go To Date dialog box. To select a date in this fashion, follow these steps:

1. Choose Go To Date from the Edit menu. Schedule+ displays the Go To Date dialog box, as shown in Figure 2-62.

FIGURE 2-62. *The Go To Date dialog box.*

2. Type in the date you want or select the portion of the date you would like to change, and click on the up arrow button or the down arrow button to scroll through the dates.

3. Choose OK.

Adding an Appointment

Schedule+ provides two ways to schedule an appointment from the appointments list. First, if the appointment is definite and does not involve others, select the date and time of the appointment and type a description of the appointment and any other information you want. If the appointment is a meeting, see the following section, titled "Scheduling Meetings." If the appointment is not a meeting and is tentative, requires a reminder, or is private, follow these steps:

1. Choose New Appointment from the Appointments menu. Schedule+ displays the Appointment dialog box, shown in Figure 2-63.

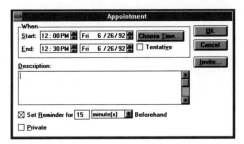

FIGURE 2-63. *The Appointment dialog box.*

2. Select the dates and times you want for the start and end of the appointment. If you select the Choose Time option, Schedule+ displays the Choose Time dialog box, shown in Figure 2-64. The Choose Time

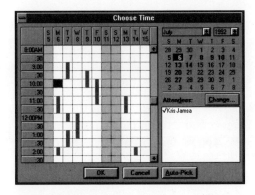

FIGURE 2-64. *The Choose Time dialog box.*

dialog box contains your weekly planner, which lets you see at a glance the time you have free. Select the time you want to set aside for your appointment and choose OK.

3. If the appointment is not yet definite, select the Tentative check box. Within your appointments list, Schedule+ indicates a tentative appointment by graying the background of the appointment description.

4. Type a description of the appointment in the Description text box. Schedule+ displays as much of the description as possible in the appointments list.

5. Select the Reminder check box to have Schedule+ display a Reminder dialog box similar to the one shown in Figure 2-65 at the time intervals you specify. Within your appointments list, Schedule+ will display a bell icon next to the appointment to let you know that you will be reminded of it.

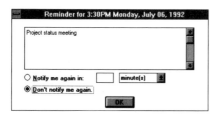

FIGURE 2-65. *A Reminder dialog box.*

6. If you don't want other users to be able to read this appointment, select the Private box. Within your appointments list, Schedule+ will indicate private appointments by using a key icon.

7. Choose OK.

Scheduling Meetings

Schedule+ makes it easy to schedule meetings. Not only does it let you see all of the attendees' schedules so that you can see when everyone is free, it also provides the means of communicating with the attendees.

Requesting a meeting

To request a meeting, follow these steps:

1. Choose the New Appointment command from the Appointments menu. Schedule+ displays the Appointment dialog box shown previously in Figure 2-63.

2. Choose the Invite button. Schedule+ displays the Select Attendees dialog box, shown in Figure 2-66.

FIGURE 2-66. *The Select Attendees dialog box.*

3. Move each attendee's name from the Directory list box to the Attendees list box by selecting it and choosing the Add button. When you finish selecting attendees, choose OK. Schedule+ adds an Attendees list box to the Appointment dialog box.

4. Choose the Choose Time button. Schedule+ displays a Choose Time dialog box similar to the one shown in Figure 2-67. The dialog box shows the times you have appointments as well as the times every other attendee has appointments. When you select a time, Schedule+ lets you know who is available at that time by placing a check mark next to the available people's names in the Attendees list box. It places an X next to unavailable people's names.

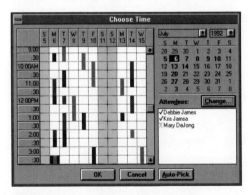

FIGURE 2-67. *The Choose Time dialog box.*

5. Select a time that is free for everyone. If you want to display the appointments for a different week, use the calendar and drop-down lists in the right side of the dialog box. If you want Schedule+ to find the first time available for everyone, specify the length of the meeting by selecting the appropriate number of squares. (Each square represents half an hour.) Then choose the Auto-Pick button. Schedule+ selects

the first available time. If you want to search for another time, choose Auto-Pick again. If you want to change the attendees list, choose the Change button. Choose OK when you've picked the time you want.

6. Type a description of the meeting in the Description text box.

7. If you want a reminder of the meeting, select the Reminder check box and specify the time that you would like to be reminded. Within your appointments list, Schedule+ will indicate that the appointment has a reminder by placing a bell icon next to the appointment.

8. Choose OK. Schedule+ displays a Send Request dialog box, as shown in Figure 2-68.

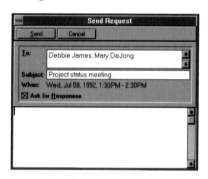

FIGURE 2-68. *The Send Request dialog box.*

9. Select the Ask For Responses check box if you want Schedule+ to prompt the attendees to respond to your request for a meeting.

10. Optionally include a short message in the text box at the bottom of the dialog box.

11. Choose Send to send the message via Mail to the Schedule+ window of each attendee.

Sending a message to meeting attendees

There may be times when you will need to inform attendees about new information or a status change. To send a message to a meeting's attendees, follow these steps:

1. Select the desired meeting in the appointments list.

2. Choose Re-Send Mail from the Appointments menu. Schedule+ displays the Send Request dialog box, shown in Figure 2-68.

3. Complete the message and choose Send to send the message to all of the attendees.

Responding to a meeting request

As other users invite you to attend meetings, you will receive messages in your Messages window describing the meeting. To respond to the meeting requests, follow these steps:

1. Make the Messages window active. Schedule+ displays your list of meeting requests and responses.

2. Double-click on the desired message to read it.

3. Choose the Accept, the Decline, or the Tentative button. (If you want to see your schedule for the meeting time, choose the View Schedule button.) If the Send Response check box is selected, Schedule+ displays a Response message to the organizer of the meeting, which indicates the button you chose. Add a note to the message if you'd like, and choose Send. If you choose Accept or Tentative, Schedule+ reserves the meeting time in your appointments list. If you choose Tentative and later decide you can attend the meeting, double-click on the meeting time in the appointments list, deselect the Tentative check box, and choose OK. Schedule+ then asks whether you want to inform the organizer that you will attend. Choose Yes, add a note to the Response message that appears, and choose Send.

Keeping track of attendee responses

If you asked for responses in a request for a meeting, you can easily see who responded and in what way by double-clicking the appointment in the appointments list to open the Appointment dialog box. The Attendee list box, which contains a list of the attendees, displays an icon before each name to indicate each person's response. If a person hasn't yet responded, Schedule+ displays a closed envelope. If a person has accepted the meeting time, you'll see a check mark. A question mark indicates a tentative response, and an X indicates a negative response.

Changing or canceling a meeting

You can change any aspect of a meeting (date, time, attendees, length, and so on) in the same way that you change aspects of an appointment. You can also cancel a meeting. See the "Editing Appointments" section below for details of how to modify or cancel a meeting. When you modify a meeting that you organized, Schedule+ asks whether you would like to notify the attendees of the change. When you modify a meeting that another person organized, Schedule+ asks whether you would like to notify the organizer of the change. Choose Yes. Schedule+ displays a message window. Add a note if you'd like, and choose Send.

Editing Appointments

Schedule+ lets you edit, reschedule, copy, or delete appointments using its Edit menu. Note that you edit meetings in the same way that you edit appointments.

Editing an appointment

To edit an appointment, follow these steps:

1. Double-click on the desired appointment, or select the desired appointment and choose Edit Appt from the Edit menu. Schedule+ displays the Appointment dialog box, shown in Figure 2-69.

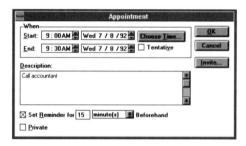

FIGURE 2-69. *The Appointment dialog box.*

2. Use the fields in the dialog box to change your appointment.

3. Choose OK.

NOTE: *You can quickly modify the length of an appointment by selecting the appointment in the appointments list and dragging the bottom border of the box surrounding the appointment to the time you want.*

Copying an appointment

To copy an appointment to another date or time, follow these steps:

1. Select the desired appointment.

2. Choose Copy Appt from the Edit menu. Schedule+ copies the appointment to the Clipboard.

3. Select the date and time to which you want to copy the appointment.

4. Choose Paste from the Edit menu.

Moving an appointment

To move an appointment to another date and time, follow these steps:

1. Select the desired appointment.

2. Choose Move Appt from the Edit menu. Schedule+ displays the Move Appointment dialog box, shown in Figure 2-70.

FIGURE 2-70. *The Move Appointment dialog box.*

3. Specify the time and date you want.

4. Choose OK.

NOTE: *You can quickly move an appointment to a different time on the same day by selecting the appointment in the appointments list and dragging the upper border of the appointment's box to the desired time.*

Deleting an appointment

To delete an appointment, follow these steps:

1. Select the appointment you want.

2. Choose Delete Appt from the Edit menu. Schedule+ deletes the appointment without asking you to verify the deletion.

Recurring Appointments

Many appointments occur on a regular basis. These are called recurring appointments. Rather than force you to repeatedly enter recurring appointments, Schedule+ lets you specify them as recurring and then schedules them for you.

Adding a recurring appointment

To add a recurring appointment to your schedule, follow these steps:

1. Choose the New Recurring Appt command from the Appointments menu. Schedule+ displays the Recurring Appointment dialog box, shown in Figure 2-71.

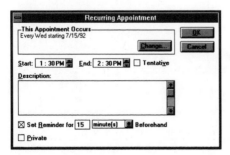

FIGURE 2-71. *The Recurring Appointment dialog box.*

2. Specify the appointment's recurrence interval by choosing the Change button. Schedule+ displays the Change Recurrence dialog box, shown in Figure 2-72. Select the interval and duration you want and choose OK.

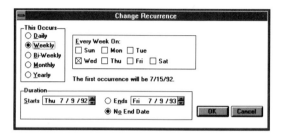

FIGURE 2-72. *The Change Recurrence dialog box.*

3. Complete the dialog box's remaining fields as discussed in the earlier section titled "Adding an Appointment."

4. Choose OK.

Within your appointments list, Schedule+ indicates recurring appointments with an icon that looks like two arrows that form a circle.

Editing or deleting a recurring appointment

To edit or delete a recurring appointment, follow these steps:

1. Choose the Edit Recurring Appts command from the Appointments menu. Schedule+ displays the Edit Recurring Appointments dialog box, shown in Figure 2-73.

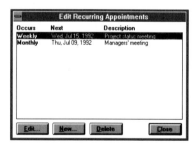

FIGURE 2-73. *The Edit Recurring Appointments dialog box.*

2. To edit an appointment, select the desired appointment and choose Edit. Schedule+ displays the Recurring Appointment dialog box, previously shown in Figure 2-71. Edit the appointment as required and choose OK. Schedule+ redisplays the Edit Recurring Appointments dialog box. Choose Close to close the dialog box.

3. To delete an appointment, select the appointment and choose Delete. Schedule+ deletes all occurrences of the appointment without asking you to verify the deletion. Choose Close to close the dialog box.

Changing Appointment Attributes

Schedule+ lets you toggle three appointment attributes with the Tentative, Private, and Set Reminder commands on the Appointments menu. A check mark next to a command means that the appointment has that attribute. Choose the Tentative command to make an appointment tentative. Choose the Private command to keep others from viewing or changing the appointment. Choose the Set Reminder command to turn on the reminder. (Edit the appointment if you want to modify the reminder time.)

If you want to turn off all reminders (including reminders for tasks), choose Turn Off Reminders from the File menu. To turn them back on, choose Turn On Reminders from the File menu.

Searching for an Appointment

There may be times when you can't remember a specific appointment's date or time. However, if you remember any part of the appointment's description, you can search for the appointment. If Schedule+ finds the text, it displays the appointments list for the day containing the appointment. To search for a specific appointment, follow these steps:

1. Choose Find from the Edit menu. Schedule+ displays the Find dialog box, shown in Figure 2-74.

FIGURE 2-74. *The Find dialog box.*

2. Type in part or all of the appointment's description. Select the direction in your calendar in which you want Schedule+ to search. Select Start Search.

3. If Schedule+ finds matching text, it displays the appointments list for the day containing the appointment.

4. If Schedule+ has found the appointment you were looking for, choose the Cancel button in the Find dialog box; otherwise, choose Find Next, and Schedule+ will resume its search.

Printing Your Appointments

Schedule+ lets you print your appointments in four different formats. The daily view displays the appointments for the day you specify. The weekly view lets you see at a glance the appointments you have in a week. The monthly view displays a calendar that gives all of the appointments in a given month. The text view lists each day within the specified time period and lists each appointment for each of those days.

To print your appointments, follow these steps:

1. Select the desired date.

2. Choose Print from the File menu. Schedule+ displays the Print dialog box, shown in Figure 2-75.

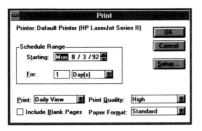

FIGURE 2-75. *The Print dialog box.*

3. Select the format you want from the Print drop-down list.

4. Specify the range of dates that you want printed in the Schedule Range box.

5. Select the paper format from the Paper Format drop-down list to modify the size of the output to fit your organizer notebook. You can choose among three formats: Standard (8½ by 11), Junior (5½ by 8), and Pocket (4 by 6½). Each is printed on 8½-by-11-inch paper, but the Junior and Pocket formats are printed on only a portion of the paper so that you can cut off the excess. You can modify the size of the formats by choosing the Setup button and changing the margin settings.

6. Choose OK.

Using the Weekly Planner

Schedule+ lets you change the display from the daily appointments list to a weekly planner. To switch between the appointments list and the weekly planner, click on the Planner tab or the Appts tab on the left side of the Schedule+ window. When you click on the Planner tab, Schedule+ displays a weekly planner that highlights your current appointments, as shown in Figure 2-76.

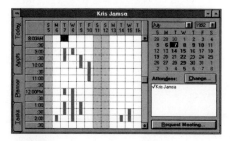

FIGURE 2-76. *The weekly planner.*

Changing the week displayed

To change the week displayed in the weekly planner, use the calendar in the upper right corner of the window. Click on a date in the week to which you want to move, or select a month and a year from the drop-down lists and then click on a date in the calendar.

Adding an appointment

To add an appointment to the weekly planner, highlight the time you would like to make the appointment for and choose New Appt from the Appointments menu. Create the appointment using the Appointment dialog box as described in the earlier section titled "Adding an Appointment."

Requesting a meeting

To set up a meeting from the weekly planner, follow these steps:

1. Choose the Change button to add attendees to the Attendees list box. Schedule+ displays the Select Attendees dialog box, shown previously in Figure 2-66. Add attendees by selecting their names and clicking on the Add button. Choose OK when you're done.

2. Schedule+ shows the schedules of all the attendees in the weekly planner window. Select a time that is free for everyone and choose Request Meeting. A Send Request message appears.

3. Type a description of the meeting in the Subject line. Add a note at the bottom of the message if you want, and choose Send. Schedule+ adds the meeting to your schedule.

Creating a Project

In addition to letting you coordinate and manage appointments, Schedule+ also lets you manage projects and their related tasks. If a task must be completed before a specific date, you can even have Schedule+ issue reminders. Before you set tasks for a project, first create a project. To create a project, follow these steps:

1. Choose New Project from the Tasks menu. Schedule+ displays the Project dialog box, shown in Figure 2-77.

FIGURE 2-77. *The Project dialog box.*

2. Type a name for the project.

3. If you want to prevent other users from viewing the tasks associated with this project, select the Private check box.

4. Choose OK.

Creating a Task

To create a task, follow these steps:

1. Choose New Task from the Tasks menu. Schedule+ displays the Task dialog box, shown in Figure 2-78.

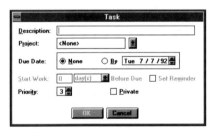

FIGURE 2-78. *The Task dialog box.*

2. Type a description of the task.

3. From the Project drop-down list, select the project to which you want the task assigned.

4. If the task has a completion date, enter the date in the Due Date box. Also indicate the number of days before the due date that you need to

start working. Select the Set Reminder check box to have Schedule+ display a reminder dialog box on the day you should start working on the task to remind you of the task's due date.

5. Select the task's priority from 1 (highest) through 9 or from A (highest) through Z.

6. If you don't want other users to be able to view this task, select the Private option.

7. Choose OK.

Viewing Your Tasks

To view your tasks, click on the Task tab, which appears on the left side of the Schedule+ window. Schedule+ displays your task list, as shown in Figure 2-79.

FIGURE 2-79. *The task list display.*

When your tasks are displayed, Schedule+ lets you add a task, change a task, delete a task, change a task's priority, mark a task as complete, or add a task to your schedule.

Adding a task

To add a task to the task list, type a description of the new task in the New Task text box and then choose Add. Schedule+ adds the task to your list with the default priority and due date. If you want to change an aspect of the task, you can edit it.

Editing a task

To edit any aspect of an existing task, double-click on the desired task, or select the desired task and choose the Edit button. Schedule+ displays the Task dialog box, previously shown in Figure 2-78. Make the desired edits and then choose OK.

Deleting a task

If a task no longer needs to be performed, delete the task by selecting it and choosing the Delete button.

Changing a task's priority

To change a task's priority, first select the desired task. Then click on the up or the down arrow displayed in the window's lower left corner to raise or lower the priority.

Marking a task as complete

When you finish a task, mark the task as complete by selecting the task and choosing the Completed button. Schedule+ removes the task from your task list. However, if you scheduled the task, it will remain in your appointments list. Schedule+ also adds a message to the Notes box in the appointments list indicating that you completed the task that day.

Scheduling a task

You might want to schedule time for your tasks so that you can be confident you will get them done. To add a task to your schedule, follow these steps:

1. Select the task you want and choose the Add To Schedule button. Schedule+ displays your weekly planner.

2. Select the date and time you want.

3. Choose OK.

Controlling the Order of Appearance in the Task List

Schedule+ lets you control the order of appearance of tasks in the task list. You can sort tasks by priority, due date, or description. To sort the task list, choose the sort order you want from the Tasks menu.

Schedule+ also lets you display all your tasks as one long list or separated by project. The View By Project command on the Tasks menu lets you toggle the current setting. If the command is preceded by a check mark, Schedule+ separates the tasks by project; otherwise, the tasks appear in one long list.

If you want to see only the tasks that you should be working on currently, choose the Show Active Tasks command from the Tasks menu. To display all tasks again, choose the Show All Tasks command.

Printing Your Tasks

Schedule+ prints your tasks in the order in which you currently have them displayed. To print your tasks, follow these steps:

1. Choose Print from the File menu. Schedule+ displays the Print dialog box, previously shown in Figure 2-75.

2. Select Tasks from the Print drop-down list.

3. Select the print quality and paper format you want.

4. Choose OK.

Editing a Project

There may be times when you want to change a project description or the project's private status. To edit a project, follow these steps:

1. If necessary, choose the View By Project command from the Tasks menu to display the project names in the task list.

2. Select the project and choose the Edit button. Schedule+ displays the Project dialog box, previously shown in Figure 2-77.

3. Edit the project as you want and choose OK.

Deleting a Project

Schedule+ lets you delete a project and the project's associated tasks all at once. To delete a project and its tasks, follow these steps:

1. If necessary, choose the View By Project command from the Tasks menu to display the project names in the task list.

2. Select the project you want to delete.

3. Choose the Delete button.

4. To confirm the deletion of the entire project, choose OK in the message box that appears.

NOTE: *If you don't want to delete specific tasks associated with a project, within the task list, drag the tasks to a different project.*

Working with Recurring Tasks

Just as you might have recurring appointments, you might also have recurring tasks. Using Schedule+, you can create, edit, and delete recurring tasks.

Creating a recurring task

To create a recurring task, follow these steps:

1. Choose New Recurring Task from the Tasks menu. Schedule+ displays the Recurring Task dialog box, shown in Figure 2-80.

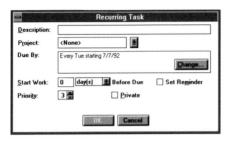

FIGURE 2-80. *The Recurring Task dialog box.*

2. Type a description of the task in the Description text box.

3. Select the task's corresponding project from the Project drop-down list.

4. Specify the task's recurrence interval by choosing the Change button. Schedule+ displays the Change Recurrence dialog box, previously shown in Figure 2-72. Select the interval you want and choose OK.

5. Complete the remaining fields as described in the earlier section titled "Adding a Task."

6. Choose OK.

Editing a recurring task

When you edit a recurring task, you can edit a single occurrence of the task or every occurrence. To edit a single occurrence, simply double-click on the task in the task list. To edit every occurrence, follow these steps:

1. Choose Edit Recurring Tasks from the Tasks menu. Schedule+ displays the Edit Recurring Tasks dialog box, shown in Figure 2-81.

FIGURE 2-81. *The Edit Recurring Tasks dialog box.*

2. Select the task you want and choose Edit. Schedule+ displays the Recurring Task dialog box, previously shown in Figure 2-80.

3. Make the edits you want and choose OK. Schedule+ redisplays the Edit Recurring Tasks dialog box.

4. Choose the Close button to close the dialog box.

Deleting a recurring task

When you delete a recurring task, you can delete a single occurrence or every occurrence. To delete a single occurrence, select the task within the task list and choose the Delete button. To delete every occurrence of a recurring task, follow these steps:

1. Choose Edit Recurring Tasks from the Tasks menu. Schedule+ displays the Edit Recurring Tasks dialog box, previously shown in Figure 2-81.

2. Select the desired task and choose the Delete button.

3. Schedule+ displays a dialog box asking whether you want to leave past occurrences of this task in the schedule. Choose Yes to keep the tasks you have already completed in your appointments list.

4. Schedule+ redisplays the Edit Recurring Tasks dialog box. Choose the Close button to close the dialog box.

Working Offline

Normally, when you work with Schedule+, you will be logged onto the network so that you can share appointment information with other users in your workgroup. However, if you are using a computer that is not connected to the network (such as a laptop PC) or if the network isn't working, you can work offline. Schedule+ disables all features that require the network. To work offline, choose the Work Offline command from the File menu.

Changing Your Password

Schedule+ uses the same password that Mail uses. You can change your password within either program. To change your password within Schedule+, follow these steps:

1. Choose Change Password from the Options menu. Schedule+ displays the Change Password dialog box, shown in Figure 2-82 on the following page.

FIGURE 2-82. *The Change Password dialog box.*

2. Type your current password in the Password text box and choose OK.

3. Type your new password in the Password text box and choose OK.

4. Repeat the new password in the Password text box and choose OK.

Viewing Another User's Schedule+ Window

Depending on the privileges another user has granted you, Schedule+ lets you read and possibly change the other user's appointments. To gain access to another user's appointments, follow these steps:

1. Choose Open Other's Appt Book from the File menu. Schedule+ displays the Open Other's Appt Book dialog box, shown in Figure 2-83.

FIGURE 2-83. *The Open Other's Appt Book dialog box.*

2. Select the user you want and choose Add.

3. Choose OK. Schedule+ opens the user's Schedule+ window. By default, it displays the appointments list. To view the weekly planner, click on the window's Planner tab. Click on the Tasks tab to see the user's task list.

4. After you are done with the user's Schedule+ window, close the window by double-clicking on its Control-menu box.

Controlling User Access to Your Schedule

To use Schedule+ to coordinate appointments with other users, you must give the other users in your workgroup some access to your schedule. You can set the amount of information to which each user can gain access. To control a user's access to your schedule, choose Set Access Privileges from the Options menu. Schedule+ displays the Set Access Privileges dialog box, shown in Figure 2-84.

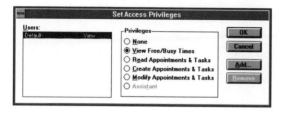

FIGURE 2-84. *The Set Access Privileges dialog box.*

Adding a user to the user list

If a user's name does not appear in the list of users and you want to provide the user a specific privilege, follow these steps:

1. Choose the Add button. Schedule+ displays the Add Users dialog box, shown in Figure 2-85.

FIGURE 2-85. *The Add Users dialog box.*

2. Select the user's name you want and choose the Add button.

3. Choose OK.

4. Select the privilege you want to give the user from the Privileges list box.

Changing a user's privileges

If the user's name currently appears in the list of users and you want to change the user's level of privilege, select the user's name, select the desired privilege, and choose OK.

Removing a user from the user list

If you want to remove a user's privileges, select the user's name and choose the Remove button.

Selecting an assistant

An assistant is a user who can manage your entire schedule. You can select only one person as an assistant. To choose an assistant, follow these steps:

1. Select the name of the assistant in the Users list box.

2. Select the Assistant privilege.

3. Choose OK.

Changing Schedule+ Display Colors

Schedule+ lets you customize the colors it uses to display different components of its window. To customize the colors, follow these steps:

1. Choose Display from the Options menu. Schedule+ displays the dialog box shown in Figure 2-86.

FIGURE 2-86. *The Display dialog box.*

2. Select the desired colors from the drop-down lists.

3. Choose OK.

Controlling Schedule+ General Options

Schedule+ lets you customize several details about its operation, such as the day you want to designate as the starting day of the week, the times your day typically begins and ends, the way in which you want to be reminded of appointments, and so on. To customize these options, follow these steps:

1. Choose General Options from the Options menu. Schedule+ displays the General Options dialog box, shown in Figure 2-87.

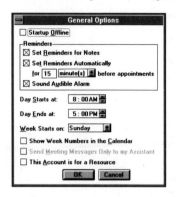

FIGURE 2-87. *The General Options dialog box.*

2. Modify any of the options you want.

3. Choose OK.

Using Schedule+ Help

Schedule+ is a very powerful program, filled with capabilities. As you work with Schedule+, you can take advantage of its help facility, which covers every topic in detail.

As with most applications for Windows, you can press F1 at any time to see context-sensitive help. You can also choose the Contents command from the Help menu to display the table of contents of the Help file for Schedule+.

Archiving Your Schedule

Over time, you will want to make backup copies (archives) of your schedule, removing past appointments. In this way, your Schedule+ file will not become too large. When you archive appointments from specific dates, Schedule+ removes them from your current Schedule+ file.

Creating an archive file

To create an archive file, follow these steps:

1. Choose Create Archive from the File menu. Schedule+ displays the Create Archive dialog box, shown in Figure 2-88.

FIGURE 2-88. *The Create Archive dialog box.*

2. Select the date before which Schedule+ will archive each appointment and choose OK. Schedule+ displays a new Create Archive dialog box, which lets you specify the name and storage place of the archive file.

3. Use the Directories and Drives boxes to specify where you would like to store the archive file. Type the name you want in the File Name box. (Click on the Network button to connect to a new drive.)

4. Choose OK. Schedule+ displays a dialog box warning you that if you archive the data, it will remove the appointments from your schedule.

6. Choose OK.

Opening an archive file

Should you ever need to open an archive file to view past appointments, follow these steps:

1. Choose Open Archive from the File menu. Schedule+ displays the Open Archive dialog box.

2. Select the archive file you want and choose OK. Schedule+ opens an appointments list containing the archived information.

3. When you finish viewing the archived appointments, close the window by double-clicking on its Control-menu box.

Importing and Exporting Appointment Files

There may be times when you will need to export a range of appointments to a file, perhaps for inclusion in a document you are preparing with your word processor. At other times, you may need to import appointments from a file.

Exporting appointments to a file

To export appointments to a file, follow these steps:

1. Choose Export Appointments from the File menu. Schedule+ displays the Export Appointments dialog box, shown in Figure 2-89.

FIGURE 2-89. *The Export Appointments dialog box.*

2. From the File Format drop-down list, select either Schedule+ or Text as the file format.

3. To export all of your appointments, select the All option button; otherwise, select the From option button and specify a range. You can specify a range only if you're exporting information to a text file.

4. Select the Include Daily Notes check box to include the daily notes from your appointments list.

5. Choose OK. Schedule+ changes the Export Appointments dialog box so that you can specify the name and location of the file. Type in the desired filename and choose OK.

Importing appointments from a file

Schedule+ lets you import appointments from files created by Schedule+, Calendar, or WordPerfect Office. To import an appointment file, follow these steps:

1. Choose Import Appointments from the File menu. Schedule+ displays the Import Appointments dialog box.

2. Select the file you want to import and choose OK. Schedule+ displays the Import Format dialog box, shown in Figure 2-90.

FIGURE 2-90. *The Import Format dialog box.*

3. Select the correct file format and select the import options you want.

4. Choose OK.

Quitting Schedule+

Schedule+ lets you quit in one of two ways. If you want to quit only Schedule+, choose Exit from the File menu. If you want to quit Schedule+ and log out of Mail at the same time, choose Exit And Sign Out from the File menu. If you are only temporarily exiting Schedule+, use the Exit option so that you won't have to later log back into Mail.

THE CLIPBOOK VIEWER

Windows uses the Clipboard—a temporary storage area in memory—to let you exchange information (either text or graphics) between applications. You can copy information to the Clipboard from one application and then paste it from the Clipboard into a second application.

Earlier versions of Windows offered an application called the Clipboard Viewer, which let you view the contents of the Clipboard, save Clipboard files, open Clipboard files, or clear the Clipboard. Windows for Workgroups includes a new application called the ClipBook Viewer, which expands the Clipboard's capabilities by being "workgroup aware." In addition to displaying the contents of your Clipboard, the ClipBook Viewer displays the contents of your ClipBook (called the local Clip-Book). The ClipBook can have many pages, each of which contains information copied from your Clipboard. You can share any page in your local ClipBook with other users in your workgroup. Similarly, you can access any shared page in anyone else's ClipBook. When you start the ClipBook Viewer, your screen displays the contents of the local Clip-Book and an icon for the Clipboard, as shown in Figure 2-91.

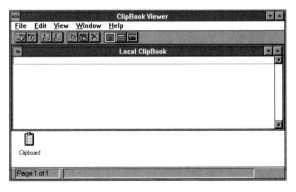

FIGURE 2-91. *The Clipboard and the local ClipBook in the ClipBook Viewer window.*

When you copy or cut information to the Clipboard, the information appears in the Clipboard window in the ClipBook Viewer. You can make the information available to other users for viewing or copying by pasting it to the local ClipBook and sharing the resulting page.

ClipBook Toolbar

To make common operations easier to perform, the ClipBook Viewer provides a toolbar with the following buttons:

Button   Action

 Connect to a remote computer's ClipBook

 Disconnect from a remote computer's ClipBook

 Share a local ClipBook page

 Stop sharing a local ClipBook page

 Copy a ClipBook page to the Clipboard

 Paste from the Clipboard to a ClipBook page

 Delete Clipboard contents or delete the selected page in the ClipBook

 Display the names of the pages in the ClipBook

 Display *thumbnails* (previews) of the pages in the ClipBook

 Display the contents of the selected page in the ClipBook

Clipboard File Operations

The ClipBook Viewer lets you save the Clipboard's current contents to a file on a disk or load a previously saved Clipboard file.

Saving Clipboard files

To save the information on the Clipboard, follow these steps:

1. Make the Clipboard window active.

2. Choose Save As from the File menu. The ClipBook Viewer displays the Save As dialog box.

3. Type the name of the file to which the information is to be saved. Use the Drives drop-down list and the Directories list box to choose the file's drive and subdirectory. (Choose Network to connect to a new network drive.)

4. Choose OK.

Opening Clipboard files

To load a previously saved Clipboard file, follow these steps:

1. Make the Clipboard window active.

2. Choose Open from the File menu. The Open dialog box appears.

3. Use the Drives drop-down list and the Directories list box to choose the file's drive and subdirectory, and then select the file in the File Name list box. (Choose Network to connect to a new network drive.)

4. Choose OK.

5. If the Clipboard currently contains some information, the ClipBook Viewer will display a dialog box asking whether you want to clear the Clipboard's contents. Choose Yes.

Accessing a Remote ClipBook

If a user of another computer in your workgroup has shared a page in his or her ClipBook, follow these steps to access the page in the remote ClipBook:

1. Click on the toolbar's Connect To Remote ClipBook button. The ClipBook Viewer displays a Select Computer dialog box similar to the one shown in Figure 2-92.

2. In the Computers list box, select the remote computer whose Clip-Book you want to access. (The list box displays both the workgroup names and the computers in the workgroups.) If you want to access a ClipBook on a computer you had connected to before, select the computer's name from the Computer Name drop-down list.

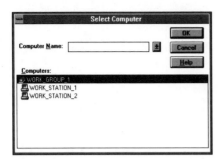

FIGURE 2-92. *The Select Computer dialog box.*

3. Choose OK.

The ClipBook Viewer displays the shared items in the remote ClipBook, as shown in Figure 2-93.

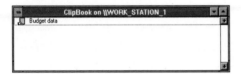

FIGURE 2-93. *A window showing the contents of a remote ClipBook.*

You can copy a page from the remote ClipBook by selecting the item and clicking on the toolbar's Copy ClipBook Page button. If the item is password protected, the ClipBook Viewer displays a dialog box prompting you for the password. Type the password and choose OK.

To disconnect from a remote ClipBook, either double-click on the remote ClipBook window's Control-menu box or make the remote Clip-Book window active and click on the toolbar's Disconnect Remote Clip-Book button.

Sharing a Local ClipBook Page

Before a remote user can access a page in your local ClipBook, you must share the item. To do so, follow these steps:

1. Select the local ClipBook page you want to share.

2. Click on the toolbar's Share Local ClipBook Page button. The Clip-Book Viewer displays the dialog box shown in Figure 2-94 on the following page.

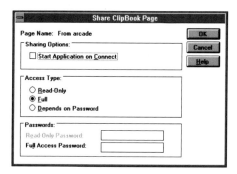

FIGURE 2-94. *The Share ClipBook Page dialog box.*

3. Select the Start Application On Connect check box to start the page's corresponding application when another computer connects to your ClipBook. This enables the creation of DDE links to documents on different computers.

4. Select the access type that controls what users in your workgroup can do with the page. Read-only access allows the user to read the page but not delete it. Full access allows the user to read and delete the page. Access that depends on a password allows the user either read-only access or full access, depending on the password entered.

5. If you select Read-Only or Full and you want to protect the page with password, type a password. If you select Depends On Password, specify two passwords: one that allows read-only access and another that allows full access.

6. Choose OK.

When you no longer want to share a page, follow these steps:

1. Select the shared local ClipBook page.

2. Click on the toolbar's Stop Sharing Local ClipBook Page button.

Moving Information Between the Clipboard and the ClipBook

The ClipBook Viewer lets you paste the Clipboard's contents to the local ClipBook or copy any page in a local or remote ClipBook to the Clipboard.

Pasting the Clipboard's contents to the local ClipBook

To paste the Clipboard's contents to the local ClipBook, follow these steps:

1. Make the local ClipBook window active.

FIGURE 2-95. *The Paste dialog box.*

2. Click on the toolbar's Paste From Clipboard button. The ClipBook Viewer displays the dialog box shown in Figure 2-95.

3. Type an item name in the Page Name text box.

4. If you want to share the item, select the Mark As Shared check box.

5. Choose OK.

Copying ClipBook contents to the Clipboard

To copy a page in your local ClipBook or in a remote ClipBook to your Clipboard, follow these steps:

1. Select the ClipBook page.

2. Click on the toolbar's Copy ClipBook Page button.

The ClipBook Viewer copies the page to the Clipboard. You can then paste the copied information into any application. If you use the Paste Link or Paste Special command to paste the item into an application that can handle DDE (dynamic data exchange), a link will be maintained with the document from which the item was originally copied. If the information in the original document is modified, the information on your machine will change as well.

Clearing the Clipboard's Contents

To clear the contents of the Clipboard, follow these steps:

1. Make the Clipboard window active.

2. Click on the toolbar's Delete button. The ClipBook Viewer displays a dialog box asking you to verify the operation. Choose Yes.

Deleting a Local ClipBook Page

To delete an item from the local ClipBook, follow these steps:

1. Select the page in the local ClipBook.

2. Click on the toolbar's Delete button. The ClipBook Viewer displays a dialog box asking you to verify the operation. Choose OK.

Controlling the ClipBook Display

The ClipBook Viewer lets you display the contents of a ClipBook window in three ways: as a list of page names, as a collection of thumbnails that show a "zoomed-out" view of each page, or as the contents of the one selected page. To control the display, make the ClipBook window active and click on one of the toolbar's display buttons: Display Names, Display Thumbnails, or Display Full Page.

Controlling the Status Bar and Toolbar Display

The ClipBook Viewer lets you toggle on or off the display of the status bar and toolbar. To do so, choose the Toolbar or the Status Bar command from the Display menu. If the command is preceded by a check mark, the Clip-Book Viewer will display the corresponding window element.

Controlling Formatting

The ClipBook Viewer lets you specify the format it uses when it displays the Clipboard contents or the contents of a single ClipBook page. An application copies information to the Clipboard in as many formats as possible to facilitate pasting that information into different applications. The ClipBook Viewer's Display menu lists all the formats copied to the Clipboard (or the ClipBook), dimming the formats that can't be displayed. The following table lists some of the common formats:

Format	Description
Default Format	Default format for the Clipboard.
Bitmap	Format for graphics that describes the image pixel by pixel.
Rich Text Format	Format for transferring text files among IBM PC, Macintosh, and XENIX/UNIX computers. It includes the text as well as some formatting information (such as bold and italic).
Native	Format for making DDE (dynamic data exchange) or OLE (object linking and embedding) connections.
OwnerLink	Format for making DDE or OLE connections.
Picture	Format for graphics that describes the image as a sequence of commands.
Text	Format for text using only characters in the Windows character set (ANSI).
Link	Format for making DDE or OLE connections.
OEM Text	Format for text that uses only characters in the MS-DOS character set (ASCII and IBM extended character sets).

To display the Clipboard contents or the ClipBook page in a different format, follow these steps:

1. Make the Clipboard window active, or select a page in a ClipBook and choose the toolbar's Display Full Page button.

2. Choose the desired format from the Display menu.

Controlling ClipBook Windows

If you open multiple remote ClipBooks, your ClipBook Viewer window can become quite cluttered. Commands in the Window menu let you tile or cascade the ClipBook windows or arrange the icons of minimized windows. In addition, you can use the menu to make a specific window the active one.

Refreshing a remote ClipBook

Because the user of a remote computer might add pages to or delete pages from the ClipBook, you should be sure to periodically update the contents of your remote ClipBook windows. To refresh the windows, choose Refresh from the Window menu or press the F5 function key.

THE PRINT MANAGER

When you print from a Windows-based application, the application sends the print file to the Print Manager. The Print Manager works in the background, sending files to the printer while you continue working. As you send files to the Print Manager, it forms a print queue—a list of files waiting to be printed.

NOTE: *When you install Windows, Setup lets you identify and configure one or more printers. If you later add or change a printer, choose the Control Panel icon from the Program Manager window, and then choose the Printers icon to inform Windows of the change.*

There are two types of print queues: *local* and *network*. A local queue is a list of files waiting to be sent to a printer attached to your computer, whereas a network queue is a list of files waiting to be printed on a network printer.

When you send files to a local queue, the Print Manager icon appears at the bottom of your desktop. By choosing this icon, you can view, rearrange, or delete files in the local print queue, as well as set several options that control how the Print Manager behaves. (Some networks don't allow you to perform these functions in a network queue.)

The Print Manager lets you connect to any printer on your network. It also enables you to share your local printer with other users in your workgroup.

Viewing Queued Files

To view the names of the files in the print queue, double-click on the Print Manager icon. The Print Manager window—similar to Figure 2-96—appears on your screen.

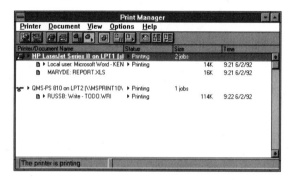

FIGURE 2-96. *The Print Manager window.*

If your computer has multiple printers attached or is connected to a network printer, information appears about each printer's queue.

Print Manager Toolbar

To make common operations easy to use, the Print Manager provides a toolbar containing the following buttons:

Button	Action
	Connect to a network printer
	Disconnect from a network printer
	Share a local printer
	Stop sharing a local printer

(continued)

continued

Button   Action

    Pause printing on the selected printer

    Resume printing on the selected printer

    Set the default printer for Windows

    Pause the selected print job

    Resume the selected print job

    Remove the selected print job

    Move the selected print job up in the queue

    Move the selected print job down in the queue

Displaying size, time, date, and status information

By default, the Print Manager displays each file's size and the time and date you sent the file to be printed. To toggle this information on and off, choose Print File Size and Time/Date Sent from the View menu. Choose the Status Text command from the View menu to control whether the Print Manager displays printer and job status text. A check mark in front of a menu command indicates that the corresponding item will be displayed.

Viewing other network queues

With some networks, the Print Manager lets you view network print queues for other printers connected to the network. To view the print queue for a network printer your computer is not connected to, use the following steps.

1. Choose Other Network Printer from the View menu. The Print Manager displays the Other Network Printer dialog box.

2. Type the name of the queue you want to see and choose View. The Print Manager displays the print jobs in the printer's queue, as shown in Figure 2-97.

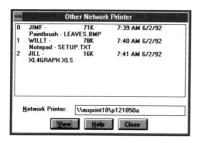

FIGURE 2-97. *The Other Network Printer dialog box.*

3. Choose Close after you finish.

Network queue status

The Print Manager periodically updates the status of network queues. The Print Manager also lets you manually update the queue status. To manually update the queue status, choose Refresh from the View menu or press F5.

Using Network Printers

The Print Manager lets you connect to network printers. When you connect to a network printer, you select a local printer port and assign the port to a network printer. (The network printer will work correctly only if you install the printer driver for the network printer's type. You can install the driver by using the Control Panel or the Printer Setup command, which is found on the Print Manager's Options menu.) When you no longer need to use the network printer, you disconnect from it.

The Print Manager enables you to transform your local printer into a network printer by sharing it. After you use the Print Manager to share it, anyone in your workgroup can use the printer.

Connecting to a network printer

To connect to a network printer, follow these steps:

1. Click on the toolbar's Connect To Network Printer button. The Print Manager displays the Connect Network Printer dialog box, shown in Figure 2-98.

FIGURE 2-98. *The Connect Network Printer dialog box.*

2. From the Device Name drop-down list, select the local port (LPT1, LPT2, LPT3, and so on) you want to use.

3. Specify the network printer to which you want to connect. First, from the Show Shared Printers On list box, select the remote computer whose printer you want to access. (The list box displays both the workgroup names and the computers in the workgroups.) Then select the printer to which you want to connect from the Shared Printers list box. If you want to connect to a printer you had connected to previously, select the printer from the Path drop-down list.

4. Choose OK.

5. If the printer is protected by a password, the Print Manager will prompt you for a password before letting you connect to the printer. Type the password and choose OK.

6. If a printer isn't installed on the port that you choose, the Print Manager displays a dialog box asking whether you want to install one. Choose Yes and use the Printers dialog box that the Print Manager displays to install a printer.

Disconnecting a network printer

To disconnect a network printer, follow these steps:

1. Click on the toolbar's Disconnect Network Printer button. The Print Manager displays the Disconnect Network Printer dialog box, shown in Figure 2-99 on the following page.

2. Select the printer to disconnect.

3. Choose OK.

FIGURE 2-99. *The Disconnect Network Printer dialog box.*

If you installed the printer before connecting, the Print Manager changes the port's printer back to a local one. If a local printer is not connected to that port on your computer, be sure you don't send any documents to the port after you've disconnected from the network printer. If you do, the Print Manager will display an error message. If you installed a printer after you specified the connection, the Print Manager removes the printer from the list.

Sharing a Local Printer

The Print Manager lets you share your local printer with other users in your workgroup.

Sharing a local printer

To share a local printer, follow these steps:

1. Click on the toolbar's Share Printer button. The Print Manager displays the Share Printer dialog box, shown in Figure 2-100.

FIGURE 2-100. *The Share Printer dialog box.*

2. From the Printer drop-down list, select the local printer you want to share.

3. Type the name by which remote users will refer to the printer when connecting to it.

4. Optionally, type a comment describing the printer. The comment appears in the Shared Printers On list box in the Connect Network Printer dialog box to help the user determine which printer to choose. After connecting to the printer, the Print Manager displays the comment in its status bar when the printer is selected.

5. If you want to protect access to the printer with a password, type the password users must specify to access the printer.

6. If you want the printer shared each time Windows starts, select the Re-share At Startup check box.

7. Choose OK.

Stopping printer sharing

To stop sharing a local printer, follow these steps:

1. Click on the toolbar's Stop Sharing Printer button. The Print Manager displays the Stop Sharing Printer dialog box, shown in Figure 2-101.

FIGURE 2-101. *The Stop Sharing Printer dialog box.*

2. Select the printer that you want to stop sharing.

3. Choose OK.

Selecting Print Job Separator Pages

Because multiple users can connect to and use your local printer, the Print Manager lets you request a separator page that it prints before each job sent to your printer. You can choose one of three types of separator page: the simple separator page, which displays the title of the print job, the user's name, and the date and time the file was printed; the standard separator page, which contains the same information as the simple page but in a larger and fancier format; and the custom separator page, the contents of which you dictate. To select a separator page, follow these steps:

1. Choose Separator Pages from the Options menu. The Print Manager displays the Separator Pages dialog box, shown in Figure 2-102.

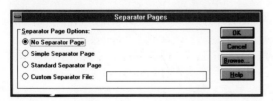

FIGURE 2-102. *The Separator Pages dialog box.*

2. Select the type of separator page you want.

3. If you selected the Custom Separator File option, type the name of the file or choose Browse to select a Windows Metafile file or a Clipboard file in the Picture format for the separator page.

4. Choose OK.

Changing the Print Queue Order

The Print Manager lets you change the order of files in print queues. On a local printer, you can move any file to any position in the print queue. On a network printer, you can move only your files, and you are limited to moving them down in the queue. To change the position of a file (job) in a print queue, drag the filename to its new position or click on the toolbar's Move Job Up button or Move Job Down button, which moves the file one position up or down in the print queue.

Removing a File from the Print Queue

To remove a file from the print queue, select its filename and click on the toolbar's Delete Job button. The Print Manager displays a dialog box asking you to confirm the deletion. Choose Yes.

NOTE: *Your network might not allow you to remove files from a network queue. If you can remove files, the Print Manager allows you to delete only files that you sent to the printer.*

Controlling the Print Manager's Priority

The Print Manager works as a background task, printing files at the same time that your computer is running other applications. To do this, your computer spends some time running applications and some time printing files. To set the priority the Print Manager uses to print jobs, follow these steps:

1. Choose Background Printing from the Options menu. The Print Manager displays the Background Printing dialog box, shown in Figure 2-103.

2. Select the desired priority.

3. Choose OK.

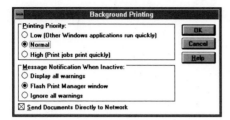

FIGURE 2-103. *The Background Printing dialog box.*

The following list describes the priority possibilities:

Priority	Result
Low	Your computer spends more time running applications than printing files. Applications run quickly, but files take a long time to print.
Normal	Your computer spends an equal amount of time running applications and printing files. This is the default setting.
High	Your computer spends more time printing files than running applications. Files print quickly, but applications might be sluggish.

Pausing and Resuming Printing

At times you might need to temporarily stop a printer from printing files. (Note that some network software does not let you stop a network printer.) Using the Print Manager, you can temporarily stop and later restart a printer, or stop and restart a print job.

Pausing and resuming printing

To pause a printer, select the printer's name and click on the toolbar's Pause Printer button.

To resume printing, select the printer's name and click on the toolbar's Resume Printer button.

Pausing and resuming a print job

To pause a print job, select the print job and click on the toolbar's Pause Print Job button.

To resume a print job, select the print job and click on the toolbar's Resume Print Job button.

Handling Printing Problems

Because it operates in the background, the Print Manager needs a way to let you know when something goes wrong (when the printer is out of paper, for example). To control how and when the Print Manager notifies you, follow these steps:

1. Choose Background Printing from the Options menu. The Print Manager displays the Background Printing dialog box, previously shown in Figure 2-103.

2. Select the desired notification technique. The following list describes the possibilities:

Command	Result
Displays all warnings	The Print Manager immediately displays a message dialog box.
Flash Print Manager window	The Print Manager beeps once and then flashes the Print Manager title bar or icon until you select the Print Manager window or enlarge the Print Manager icon.
Ignore all warnings	The Print Manager ignores the problem. (The printer status is changed to *stalled*. You'll see a message only if you make the Print Manager window active.)

Printing Network Jobs Directly

When you print to a network printer, by default the job bypasses the Print Manager and goes directly to the network queue. If you prefer, you can have the Print Manager handle the print jobs you send to a network printer. To control the Print Manager's role in network printing, follow these steps:

1. Choose Background Printing from the Options menu. The Print Manager displays the Background Printing dialog box, previously shown in Figure 2-103.

2. To bypass the Print Manager, select the Send Jobs Directly To Network check box. If you want the Print Manager to oversee network printing, deselect the check box.

Customizing the Print Manager

The Print Manager lets you toggle the display of the status bar and the toolbar. It also lets you select the font used to display the queue and file status information.

Controlling the status bar display

To toggle the display of the status bar, choose Status Bar from the Options menu. If a check mark appears beside the command in the menu, the status bar is displayed.

Controlling the toolbar display

To toggle the display of the toolbar, choose Toolbar from the Options menu. If a check mark appears beside the command in the menu, the toolbar is displayed.

Selecting a font

To select the font used by the Print Manager to display queue and file status information, follow these steps:

1. Choose Font from the Options menu. The Print Manager displays the Font dialog box, shown in Figure 2-104.

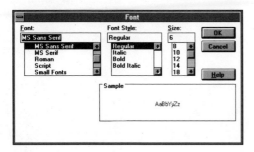

FIGURE 2-104. *The Font dialog box.*

2. Select the font, style, and size you want.

3. Choose OK.

Selecting the Default Windows Printer

The Print Manager lets you select a printer as the default one used by applications in Windows unless you specify otherwise. To select the default printer, follow these steps:

1. Select the name of the printer you want to make the default.

2. Click on the toolbar's Set Default Printer button.

Closing the Print Manager

To close the Print Manager, double-click on its Control-menu box or choose Exit from the Printer menu. Closing the Print Manager deletes all files in all local print queues, so the Print Manager displays a dialog box asking you to confirm the deletions.

THE TASK LIST

Windows lets you run several applications at the same time, each within its own window. To move among these windows quickly, you can either click in the window to which you want to move or use the Task List.

Activating the Task List

To activate the Task List, double-click anywhere on the desktop (outside of windows and away from icons), or press Ctrl+Esc. A dialog box similar to the one shown in Figure 2-105 appears.

FIGURE 2-105. *The Task List dialog box.*

Using the Task List

To switch to an application, simply double-click on the desired application name, or use the arrow keys to select the application name and then choose Switch To.

Stopping Applications with the Task List

You can also use the Task List to stop an application. Select the name of the application, and choose End Task. If the application has open documents, Windows prompts you to save the changes.

Canceling the Task List

After you finish using the Task List, click on Cancel or press Esc.

THE PIF EDITOR

The more Windows knows about the way a program operates, the better Windows integrates that application into the Windows environment with the rest of your applications. Applications designed for Windows automatically supply Windows with the information that it needs, but applications not designed for Windows (such as MS-DOS–based applications) do not.

A *program information file* (*PIF*) provides Windows with key information it needs to know about applications not designed for Windows. In most cases, you don't need to create a PIF for these types of applications; Windows provides a default PIF that is normally sufficient. If you want to provide Windows with more specific information about an application not designed for Windows, however, you can create a PIF using the PIF Editor. Depending on the mode in which you're running Windows, the steps you perform—and the information you provide— differ. In both standard mode and 386 enhanced mode, however, you perform the following operations.

Creating a PIF

To create a PIF for an application not designed for Windows, follow these steps:

1. Double-click on the PIF Editor icon in the Main group window.
2. Set all fields as desired. (Standard mode fields are covered later in the section titled "Standard Mode." 386 enhanced mode fields are covered in the section titled "386 Enhanced Mode" below.)
3. After you complete all fields, choose Save As from the File menu.
4. Type the filename that matches the application's name but has the extension .PIF, and choose OK.

Editing an Existing PIF

To edit an existing PIF, follow these steps:

1. Double-click on the PIF Editor icon in the Main group window.
2. Choose Open from the File menu.
3. Type the name of the file, or select the file using the File Name and Directories list boxes and the Drives drop-down list.
4. Set all fields as desired. (Standard mode fields are covered in the section below titled "Standard Mode." 386 enhanced mode fields are covered in the section below titled "386 Enhanced Mode.")
5. Choose Save from the File menu.

Standard Mode

When you run the PIF Editor in standard mode, a PIF Editor window similar to the one shown in Figure 2-106 appears.

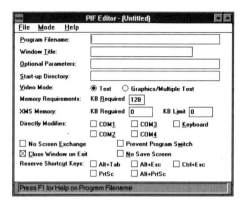

FIGURE 2-106. *A PIF Editor window in standard mode.*

The following paragraphs describe each standard mode PIF field:

- *Program Filename* specifies the application's complete pathname (drive, directory, filename, and extension). If the application is in your computer's search path (as listed in your computer's AUTOEXEC.BAT file), you need only enter the application's name and extension.

- *Window Title* specifies the parameters for the name you want to appear in the application's title bar or beneath the application's icon when it is minimized. Typically, you use the application's name.

- *Optional Parameters* specifies the parameters for the application's command line. If you use the question mark (?), Windows displays a dialog box before the application runs to prompt you for the parameters.

- *Start-up Directory* directs Windows to change to the directory specified before running the application. If you don't specify a directory, Windows uses the application's directory.

- *Video Mode* specifies the video mode in which the application runs. If you are not sure of the video mode that is used, select Graphics/ Multiple Text.

- *Memory Requirements* tells Windows the minimum amount of conventional memory (in KB) the application needs.

■ *XMS Memory* has two fields: KB Required and KB Limit. KB Required specifies the amount of extended memory (in KB) the application needs. KB Limit specifies the maximum amount of extended memory Windows lets the application use.

■ *Directly Modifies* tells Windows what devices the application modifies, letting Windows restrict the devices' use by other applications.

■ *No Screen Exchange* prevents you from copying the application's screen onto the Clipboard using the Print Screen key and the Alt+Print Screen key combination. The only reason to select this option is to provide a small amount of extra memory to the application.

■ *Prevent Program Switch* lets Windows save a small amount of memory by preventing you from switching from this application to another. When this option is selected, you can return to Windows only by exiting the application.

■ *Close Window on Exit* directs Windows to close the application's window when the application ends, as opposed to displaying the application's ending screen and prompting you with the message *Hit Any Key to Exit.*

■ *No Save Screen* directs Windows not to save a copy of a program designed for MS-DOS's screen when you switch to another application. The application's screen might not be restored correctly when you return to it.

■ *Reserve Shortcut Keys* directs Windows to reserve the specified key combinations for the application's use, instead of treating the key combinations as predefined Windows shortcut keys.

386 Enhanced Mode

When you run the PIF Editor in 386 enhanced mode, a PIF Editor window similar to the one shown in Figure 2-107 on the following page appears.

The following paragraphs describe each 386 enhanced mode PIF field:

■ *Program Filename* specifies the application's complete pathname (drive, directory, filename, and extension). If the application is in your computer's search path (as listed in your computer's AUTOEXEC.BAT file), you need only enter the application's name and extension.

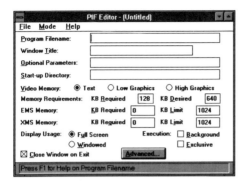

FIGURE 2-107. *A PIF Editor window in 386 enhanced mode.*

■ *Window Title* specifies the name you want to appear in the application's title bar or beneath the application's icon when it is minimized. Typically, you use the application's name.

■ *Optional Parameters* specifies the parameters for the application's command line. If you use the question mark (?), Windows displays a dialog box before the application runs to prompt you for the parameters.

■ *Start-up Directory* directs Windows to change to the directory specified before running the application. If you don't specify a directory, Windows uses the application's directory.

■ *Video Memory* specifies how much memory Windows reserves to save the application's window when it switches between tasks. If the application uses text mode, select Text. If the application uses CGA graphics mode, select Low Graphics. If the application uses EGA or VGA graphics mode, select High Graphics.

■ *Memory Requirements* has two fields: KB Required and KB Desired. KB Required specifies the minimum amount of conventional memory the application needs. KB Desired specifies the maximum amount of conventional memory Windows lets the application use. The only reason to change this entry is to reserve more memory for other applications.

■ *EMS Memory* has two fields: KB Required and KB Limit. KB Required specifies the minimum amount of expanded memory the application needs. KB Limit specifies the maximum amount of expanded memory Windows lets the application use.

■ *XMS Memory* has two fields: KB Required and KB Limit. KB Required specifies the minimum amount of extended memory that the application needs. KB Limit specifies the maximum amount of extended memory Windows lets the application use.

■ *Display Usage* has two option buttons: Full Screen and Windowed. Full Screen specifies that the application runs full screen; Windowed specifies that the application runs in a window. Windows lets you toggle the display of an application not designed for Windows between full screen and a window by pressing Alt+Enter.

■ *Execution* contains two check boxes: Background and Exclusive. If you select Background, Windows allows the application to run in the background while you use another application. If you deselect Background, Windows stops running the application when you switch to another application. Selecting Exclusive tells Windows to suspend execution of all other applications while the application controlled by this PIF is running in the foreground—even if the other applications have their Background option selected. The advantage of this option is that the application controlled by this PIF runs faster and has access to more memory.

■ *Close Window on Exit* directs Windows to close the application's window when the application ends, as opposed to displaying the application's ending screen and prompting you with the message *Hit Any Key to Exit.*

At the bottom of the dialog box is a button labeled Advanced. Choosing Advanced brings up a second dialog box, similar to the one shown in Figure 2-108.

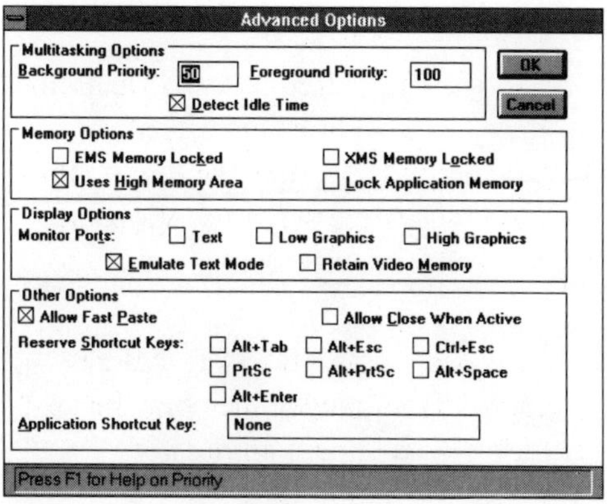

FIGURE 2-108. *The Advanced Options dialog box.*

The following paragraphs briefly describe the fields in this dialog box:

- *Background Priority* and *Foreground Priority* control the amount of time Windows spends running the application when the application is running in the background or in the foreground. Priority values range from 0 through 10,000. These values are meaningful only when compared to other applications.

  For example, suppose three applications are running. The application in the foreground has a foreground priority of 100, and each of the two applications in the background has a background priority of 50. Therefore, the total priority for all applications is 200. The percentage of time Windows spends running each application is equal to the application's priority divided by the total priority of all applications. Therefore, the foreground application is running 50 percent of the time (100 ÷ 200), and each background application is running 25 percent of the time (50 ÷ 200).

- *Detect Idle Time* directs Windows to let other applications run while an application is idle, waiting for your input.

- *EMS Memory Locked* prevents Windows from swapping the contents of the application's expanded memory to disk. This increases the application's performance but decreases overall Windows performance.

- *XMS Memory Locked* prevents Windows from swapping the contents of the application's extended memory to disk. This increases the application's performance but decreases overall Windows performance.

- *Uses High Memory Area* tells Windows that the application can use the high memory area (the first 64 KB of extended memory).

- *Lock Application Memory* prevents Windows from swapping the program to disk. This increases the application's performance but decreases overall Windows performance.

- The *Monitor Ports* check boxes specify the video mode in which the application will run. When you select a check box, Windows verifies that the application's display adapter values are correct for the video mode. This helps to prevent problems that can occur when an application directly interacts with your computer's display adapter. If your application's display looks normal, don't modify these settings because doing so will slow down the application significantly.

■ If your display doesn't look normal, select the option button that corresponds to the video mode the application runs in (Text for text mode, Low Graphics for CGA graphics mode, and High Graphics for EGA or VGA graphics mode).

■ *Emulate Text Mode* lets Windows quickly display an application's text output. Leave this option selected unless the application's display doesn't look normal.

■ *Retain Video Memory* directs Windows not to reduce the amount of memory used for an application's display when the application is running. This prevents the application from losing video memory when you switch to another graphics mode.

■ *Allow Fast Paste* lets Windows paste text from the Clipboard into the application as fast as possible. If an application has difficulties with paste operations, disable this option.

■ *Allow Close When Active* allows Windows to close an active application automatically when you exit Windows.

■ *Reserve Shortcut Keys* directs Windows to reserve the specified key combinations for use by the application instead of treating the key combinations as predefined Windows shortcut keys.

■ *Application Shortcut Key* lets you specify a key or key combination that makes the application the foreground task.

PART III

Customizing and Optimizing Windows with the Control Panel

Windows lets you customize several features, ensuring that your computer suits your needs and provides a comfortable working environment. This section shows you how to take advantage of the versatility Windows offers.

At the heart of Windows customization is the *Control Panel.* The Control Panel provides you with a variety of options that let you set up Windows in the way that works best for you.

To use the Control Panel, double-click on the Control Panel icon in the Program Manager window. The window shown in Figure 3-1 appears.

FIGURE 3-1. *The Control Panel and its options.*

Control Panel options appear as icons within the Control Panel window. These options perform the following tasks:

Change screen colors (*Color*)   Set date and time (*Date/Time*)

Manage fonts (*Fonts*)   Modify network options (*Network*)

(continued)

continued

Configure serial ports (*Ports*)

Customize mouse (*Mouse*)

Customize desktop (*Desktop*)

Set keyboard response (*Keyboard*)

Configure printers (*Printers*)

Specify international settings (*International*)

Select MIDI setup for sound device (*MIDI Mapper*)

Disable warning beeps (*Sound*)

Specify which applications have priority (*386 Enhanced*)

Managing drivers for sound cards and CD-ROMs (*Drivers*)

Windows displays explanatory text at the bottom of the Control Panel window that describes the current option. If you click on an option or select an option using the arrow keys, Windows displays explanatory text for that option. The following sections describe how to use each of the Control Panel's options.

CHANGING SCREEN COLORS

The Color option lets you change the colors used for different areas of the screen, such as the desktop, window background, window borders, window title bar, and so on. When you choose the Color option, a dialog box similar to the one shown in Figure 3-2 appears.

FIGURE 3-2. *The Color dialog box.*

This dialog box represents the different areas of your desktop—windows, window borders, title bars, and so on. As you select different colors, you see how the colors will appear on your screen by looking at the model of the screen inside the dialog box.

Using a Predefined Color Scheme

Windows comes with several predefined color combinations. To use a predefined color combination, follow these steps:

1. Open the Color Schemes drop-down list.

2. Select a color scheme from the list. The colors in the dialog box change to reflect your selection.

3. When you see a color scheme you like, choose OK. Windows adopts the new color scheme.

Changing the Color of a Screen Element

To change the color of a particular screen element, such as window title bars or scroll bars, follow these steps:

1. Choose the Color Palette button. Windows expands the Color dialog box, as shown in Figure 3-3.

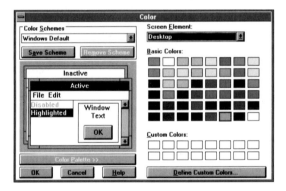

FIGURE 3-3. *The Color dialog box with palette.*

2. Open the Screen Element drop-down list, and select the screen element whose color you want to change. You can also select the screen element you want to change by clicking on the element's representation on the left side of the dialog box.

3. Select the new color, and choose OK.

Creating a Color

The Color option also lets you create your own colors. To do so, follow these steps:

1. Move to the Custom Colors field, and select a box for the new color.

2. Choose Define Custom Colors. A dialog box similar to the one shown in Figure 3-4 appears.

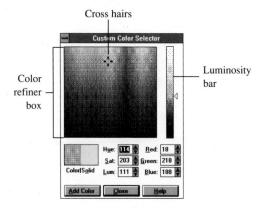

FIGURE 3-4. *The Custom Color Selector dialog box.*

3. Select the color you want. First click within the color refiner box to move the cross hairs to the desired color scheme. Then adjust the brightness of the color by dragging the arrow at the right of the luminosity bar. The Color|Solid box reflects your current selection. You can further adjust the color by changing the values in the boxes beneath the color refiner box. The following diagram shows how these numbers are interpreted in the color refiner box.

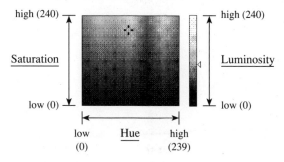

4. Choose Add Color.

5. Choose Close.

MANAGING FONTS

A *font* is a complete set of typographic characters of a certain size. A *font file* is a file that contains a font. When you purchase a new font file, you add it to Windows so that you can use it. When you choose the

Fonts icon in the Control Panel window, a dialog box similar to the one shown in Figure 3-5 appears.

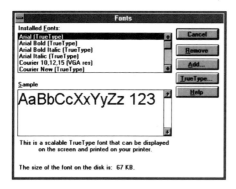

FIGURE 3-5. *The Fonts dialog box.*

Adding a Font

To add a font, follow these steps:

1. Double-click on the Fonts icon in the Control Panel window.

2. Choose Add. A dialog box similar to the one shown in Figure 3-6 appears.

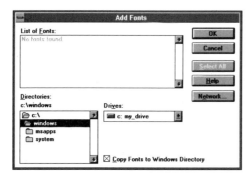

FIGURE 3-6. *The Add Fonts dialog box.*

3. Open the Drives drop-down list and select the drive that contains the font file. (Choose the Network button to connect to a new network drive.)

4. In the Directories box, select the directory containing the font file.

5. Select the font in the List Of Fonts list box.

6. Choose OK.

Removing a Font

To remove a font, follow these steps:

1. Double-click on the Fonts icon in the Control Panel window.

2. From the Installed Fonts list box, select the font you want to remove.

3. Choose Remove.

4. A second dialog box appears, asking you to confirm the font removal. Choose Yes to remove the font, or choose No to cancel the procedure.

Using TrueType Fonts

A TrueType font is a scalable font that prints exactly as it appears on your screen. You can control whether Windows uses TrueType fonts and whether it uses them exclusively. To use TrueType fonts, follow these steps:

1. Choose TrueType in the Fonts dialog box. The TrueType dialog box shown in Figure 3-7 appears.

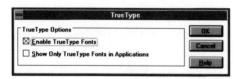

FIGURE 3-7. *The TrueType dialog box.*

2. Select the Enable TrueType Fonts check box to let Windows use TrueType fonts.

3. Select the Show Only TrueType Fonts In Applications check box to make Windows use only TrueType fonts.

4. Choose OK.

CONFIGURING SERIAL PORTS

Serial ports let you connect a mouse, a modem, or another hardware device to your computer. As part of the connection process, you set the communication parameters of each serial port to match the parameters of the device. (The manual for your hardware device describes its parameters.) To do so, double-click on the Ports icon in the Control Panel window. The dialog box in Figure 3-8 on the following page appears.

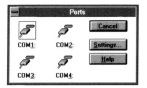

FIGURE 3-8. *The Ports dialog box.*

To set a port's communication parameters, follow these steps:

1. Select the desired port.

2. Choose Settings. A dialog box similar to the one shown in Figure 3-9 appears.

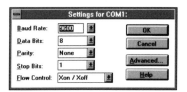

FIGURE 3-9. *The Settings dialog box.*

3. Select the desired baud rate, number of data bits, parity, number of stop bits, and the method of flow control from the drop-down lists.

4. After you finish setting the port's communication parameters, choose OK. Choose Close in the Ports dialog box.

Communications Terminology

To set up ports, you need to be familiar with the following terms in the Ports dialog box:

Baud rate The speed with which information is transferred through the port.

Data bits The number of bits used for each character.

Parity The method of error checking that both devices agree to use.

Stop bits The amount of time between transmitted characters. (One stop bit is the time necessary to transmit one bit.)

Flow control The method used to control the flow of data.

CUSTOMIZING THE MOUSE

If you have a mouse, you can use the Control Panel's Mouse icon to control how fast the mouse pointer moves and how fast you double-click to choose items. You can even swap the actions of the left and right mouse buttons (a handy option for left-handed mouse users).

To customize your mouse, double-click on the Mouse icon in the Control Panel window. A dialog box similar to the one shown in Figure 3-10 appears.

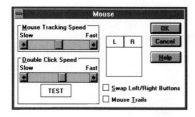

FIGURE 3-10. *The Mouse dialog box.*

To set mouse tracking speed (the speed at which the mouse cursor moves across the screen), simply drag the Mouse Tracking Speed scroll box to the desired area in the scroll bar.

To set the double-click speed, simply drag the Double-Click Speed scroll box to the desired area in the scroll bar. To test the double-click speed, double-click on the box labeled *TEST.* If the box changes color, your double-click was fast enough to choose an item.

To swap the functions of the left and right mouse buttons, select the Swap Left/Right Buttons check box.

Selecting the Mouse Trails check box improves the visibility of the mouse pointer on LCD screens. The Mouse Trails option gives an accordion effect to your mouse pointer. When you move the pointer, an ''accordion'' of arrows trails behind the pointer. When you stop the pointer's movement, the trailing arrows catch up to and merge with the pointer.

Choose OK after you finish customizing your mouse.

CUSTOMIZING YOUR DESKTOP

The default Windows desktop, although fully functional, is rather impersonal. You can, however, change the look of the desktop, the width of window borders, the cursor blink rate, and other items. To do so, double-click on the Desktop icon in the Control Panel window. A dialog box similar to the one in Figure 3-11 on the following page appears.

FIGURE 3-11. *The Desktop dialog box.*

Selecting a Background Pattern

By default, your desktop is a solid color. You can change the desktop to
a predefined background pattern, create your own background pattern,
or even use a graphics file created by Paintbrush or a similar
application.

Windows provides several predefined background patterns, as shown in
Figure 3-12.

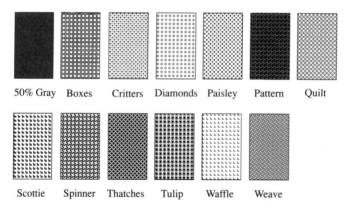

FIGURE 3-12. *Predefined background patterns.*

To use a predefined background pattern, follow these steps:

1. Open the Name drop-down list from the Pattern field.

2. Choose a background pattern.

3. Choose OK.

Creating Your Own Pattern

NOTE: *You need a mouse to create your own background pattern. You cannot create your own background pattern from the keyboard.*

If none of the predefined background patterns suits your tastes, you can create your own. To do so, follow these steps:

1. Choose Edit Pattern from the Pattern field. A dialog box similar to the one shown in Figure 3-13 appears.

FIGURE 3-13. *The Desktop - Edit Pattern dialog box.*

2. Type in a name for your pattern, but do *not* press Enter.

3. Click inside the large center box. A large black square appears. Click on the square, and it disappears. The Sample box shows what the pattern looks like on the desktop.

   □ To paint, click on a blank area and drag.

   □ To erase, click on a filled area and drag.

4. After you finish editing, choose Add.

5. Choose OK.

Editing an Existing Pattern

NOTE: *You need a mouse to edit a background pattern. You cannot edit a background pattern from the keyboard.*

To save time, you can also edit an existing background pattern. To do so, follow these steps:

1. Open the Name drop-down list from the Pattern field in the Desktop dialog box.

2. Select the pattern you want to edit.

3. Choose Edit Pattern. The Desktop - Edit Pattern dialog box appears with the pattern you selected.

4. Click inside the large center box. A large black square appears. Click on the square, and it disappears. The Sample box shows what the pattern looks like on the desktop.

5. If you want to keep the original pattern and save the edited pattern under a new name, type the new name in the Name field and choose Add. If you want to replace the original pattern with the edited one, choose Change.

6. Choose OK.

Deleting a Pattern

To delete a pattern, follow these steps:

1. Open the Name drop-down list in the Desktop dialog box from the Pattern field.

2. Select the pattern you want to remove.

3. Choose Edit Pattern.

4. Choose Remove.

5. A dialog box asks you to confirm the deletion. Choose Yes to remove the pattern, or choose No to cancel the procedure.

6. Choose OK.

Selecting Wallpaper

When it comes to customizing your desktop, you're not limited to background patterns. You can also use *wallpaper* (a graphics image) to add an interesting flair. Windows provides several predefined wallpapers, one of which is the Windows logo, shown in Figure 3-14. The following table describes the wallpapers that come with Windows.

Wallpaper	Description
256COLOR.BMP	Colored balls and their shadows, in 256 colors
ARCADE.BMP	Marbled gray and green diamonds
ARGYLE.BMP	Blue and pink argyle
CARS.BMP	Parked cars
CASTLE.BMP	Gray bricks
EGYPT.BMP	Interlocking geometric pattern
HONEY.BMP	Honeycomb
LEAVES.BMP	Autumn leaves
REDBRICK.BMP	Red bricks

(continued)

continued

Wallpaper	Description
RIVETS.BMP	Blue rivets
SQUARES.BMP	Purple three-dimensional squares
THATCH.BMP	Gray weave pattern
WINLOGO.BMP	Logo for Windows
ZIGZAG.BMP	Purple diagonal zigzags

FIGURE 3-14. *One of several available wallpapers.*

To select a wallpaper, follow these steps in the Desktop dialog box:

1. Under Wallpaper, open the File drop-down list.

2. Select the filename representing the wallpaper you want.

3. Select either Center or Tile. Center centers the wallpaper on your desktop. Tile repeats the wallpaper as many times as necessary to completely cover your desktop.

NOTE: *The wallpaper appears after you close the Desktop dialog box.*

4. Choose OK.

Creating your own wallpaper

To create your own wallpaper, follow these steps:

1. Use the Paintbrush accessory to draw the wallpaper.

2. Save the file as a bitmap file (with the extension BMP).

If you copy the file to the Windows subdirectory, the next time you open the Desktop dialog box, your file will be listed in the File list box. If you don't save the wallpaper file in the Windows subdirectory, you can select it by specifying its full pathname in the File drop-down list.

You should keep a few factors in mind when creating your wallpaper in Paintbrush. By default, Paintbrush presents a painting area that is 640 pixels by 442 pixels. If you want to create a picture that fills the screen, you should make the size of the painting area match the size of your screen. To do so, choose Image Attributes from the Options menu, select the Pels option button, and change the values in the Width and Height text boxes to match the dimensions of your screen. (The default VGA screen is 640 pixels by 480 pixels.) Also notice that when you choose Save from the File menu, Paintbrush saves the entire painting area. If you're creating a small picture that you will use as a tile in a wallpaper pattern that fills the screen, save only the picture, not the entire painting area; otherwise your wallpaper will contain your picture and a lot of white space. After you draw your picture, select it with the Pick tool, choose Copy To from the Edit menu, specify the name of the file, and choose OK. Paintbrush saves only the selected picture to the file.

Using Fast Alt+Tab Switching

Fast Alt+Tab switching is a method of quickly switching between running applications. To enable Fast Alt+Tab switching, select the Fast Alt+Tab Switching check box in the Desktop dialog box.

To use Fast Alt+Tab switching, hold down the Alt key and press Tab (while continuing to hold down the Alt key). Windows draws a rectangle in the middle of the screen that contains the icon of a running application. Press Tab again (while continuing to hold down the Alt key), and the icon of the next running application appears. Keep pressing Tab until you see the icon of the application to which you'd like to switch, and then release the Alt key.

Selecting a Screen Saver

Screen savers prevent the monitor from permanently burning in a screen image, damaging your screen display. You can have the screen-saver software display random or changing images while you are not working with the system. Windows provides several screen savers, each of which displays a different image.

Screen Saver	Image
Blank Screen	Blanks the screen display
Flying Windows	Displays a screenful of Windows icons that start small and grow as they appear to move toward you
Marquee	Displays scrolling text on a blank background
Starfield Simulation	Displays a simulation of flight through a starfield

To select a screen saver, open the Name drop-down list and select the screen saver you want.

The Delay option lets you specify the amount of time that elapses before the screen saver appears if you are not moving the mouse or pressing any keys. To change the delay, click on the up or down arrow to increase or decrease the amount of time, or type in the desired delay, from 0 through 99 minutes.

With the exception of Blank Screen, each screen saver can be customized to suit your own taste.

Setting up Flying Windows

To set up the Flying Windows screen saver, follow these steps:

1. Select Flying Windows and choose Setup. A dialog box similar to the one shown in Figure 3-15 appears.

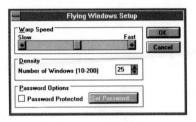

FIGURE 3-15. *The Flying Windows Setup dialog box.*

2. Select the speed at which the Windows icons move and the number of Windows icons displayed.

3. If you'd like to use password protection, see the section on passwords below.

4. Choose OK.

Setting up Marquee

To set up the Marquee screen saver, follow these steps:

1. Select Marquee and choose Setup. A dialog box similar to the one shown in Figure 3-16 appears. Pay attention to the Text Example box; it demonstrates the result of your customizations.

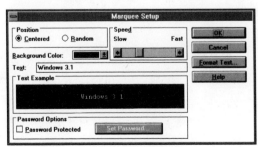

FIGURE 3-16. *The Marquee Setup dialog box.*

2. If you want the text to scroll across the middle of the screen, select Centered. For text to scroll at random heights from the bottom of the screen, select Random.

3. Select the speed at which the text scrolls.

4. Select the background color from the Background Color drop-down list.

5. Type the text you want displayed in the Text text box. If you'd like to format the text, choose Format Text. A dialog box similar to the one shown in Figure 3-17 appears. The Sample box demonstrates the results of the formatting.

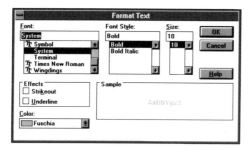

FIGURE 3-17. *The Format Text dialog box.*

6. Select the text's font, style, and size from the Font, Font Style, and Size list boxes.

7. Select any text effects you want from the Effects box.

8. Select the text's color in the Color drop-down list.

9. Choose OK when the text is formatted the way you want.

10. If you'd like to use password protection, see the section on passwords below.

11. Choose OK.

Setting up Starfield Simulation

To set up the Starfield Simulation screen saver, follow these steps:

1. Select Starfield Simulation and choose Setup. A dialog box similar to the one shown in Figure 3-18 appears.

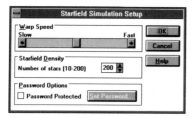

FIGURE 3-18. *The Starfield Simulation Setup dialog box.*

2. Use the Warp Speed scroll bar to select the speed at which the stars move.

3. Use the Starfield Density area to select the number of stars.

4. If you'd like to use password protection, see the section on passwords below.

5. Choose OK.

Setting passwords

When password protection is enabled, you can't return to Windows from a screen saver without typing the password. To use password protection, follow these steps:

1. Select the Password Protection check box in the screen saver's Setup dialog box.

2. Choose Set Password. A dialog box similar to the one shown in Figure 3-19 appears.

FIGURE 3-19. *The Change Password dialog box.*

3. If you've previously set a password, type the old password in the Old Password text box. (This helps prevent someone from altering your password.)

4. Type the password you desire in the New Password text box.

5. Type the password again in the Retype New Password text box. (This is a safety check to make sure you typed the password correctly the first time.)

6. Choose OK.

Changing the Icon Spacing

Icon spacing is the distance (in pixels) Windows places between icons. Click on the up or down arrow in the Spacing box in the Desktop dialog box to increase or decrease the value for icon spacing.

Select the Wrap Title check box to allow Windows to display long icon names on two lines.

Using the Sizing Grid Box

The Sizing Grid box in the Desktop dialog box contains two fields. The first, *Granularity,* lets you set the size of the grid Windows uses to position windows and icons on the desktop. The second, *Border Width,* lets you set the size of the window borders.

To change the granularity or the window border width, click on the up or down arrow in the Granularity or Border Width text box to increase or decrease the number.

Changing the Cursor Blink Rate

To increase or decrease the rate at which your cursor blinks, click on the left or right arrow in the Cursor Blink Rate scroll bar in the Desktop dialog box to make the cursor blink rate a little slower or faster, or drag the scroll box to rapidly change the rate. The sample cursor to the right of the scroll bar blinks at the rate you choose.

SETTING THE KEYBOARD RESPONSE

Keyboard response is controlled by two factors: how long your computer waits after you press a key to repeat the character of that key, and how quickly a held-down key repeats its character. To change the keyboard response, double-click on the Keyboard icon in the Control Panel window. A dialog box similar to the one shown in Figure 3-20 appears.

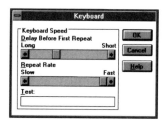

FIGURE 3-20. *The Keyboard dialog box.*

To change the delay before a pressed key repeats its character, click on the left or right arrow in the Delay Before First Repeat scroll bar to increase or decrease the delay, or drag the scroll box to the left or to the right.

To change the key repeat rate, click on the left or right arrow in the Repeat Rate scroll bar to make the key repeat rate a little slower or a little faster, or drag the scroll box to rapidly change the key repeat rate.

To test the keyboard response, select the Test text box and hold down a key. When you're satisfied with the keyboard response, choose OK.

CONFIGURING A PRINTER

If you add or change a printer, you use the Printers option to inform Windows of the change. When you double-click on the Printers icon in the Control Panel window, a dialog box similar to the one shown in Figure 3-21 appears.

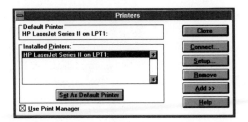

FIGURE 3-21. *The Printers dialog box.*

NOTE: *You can use the Print Manager to perform all of the operations described in this section. See "The Print Manager" in Part II.*

Adding a Printer

To add a printer, follow these steps:

1. Choose the Add button. The dialog box changes to look similar to the one shown in Figure 3-22.

2. Select the desired printer from the List of Printers list box.

3. Choose Install.

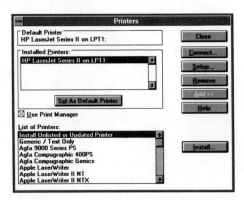

FIGURE 3-22. *The Printers dialog box with a list of available printers.*

4. A dialog box that tells you to insert the disk containing the required printer driver appears. Insert the requested disk into the disk drive, and choose OK. (You can type a different drive letter and path in the text box, if necessary.)

Connecting a Printer to a Port

Before you can print, you must identify the port to which your printer is attached. Follow these steps:

1. Select the printer to which you want to connect from the Installed Printers list box in the Printers dialog box.

2. Choose Connect. A dialog box similar to the one shown in Figure 3-23 appears.

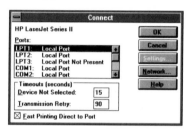

FIGURE 3-23. *The Connect dialog box.*

3. Select a port for the printer, and then choose OK.

NOTE: *If you need to set specific printer options for the printer to which you're connecting, choose Setup in the Printers dialog box. A dialog box with options specific to the selected printer appears. Depending on your printer, you might be able to select a paper source, a paper size, and the number of copies to print. Some printers even let you scale high-resolution graphics and change the orientation of the page. See your printer's manual for the proper settings for these options.*

Connecting to and Disconnecting a Network Printer

Use the Connect Network Printer dialog box to connect to and disconnect a network printer. To open the dialog box, follow these steps:

1. Choose the printer in the Installed Printers list box in the Printers dialog box.

2. Choose Connect. A dialog box similar to the one previously shown in Figure 3-23 appears.

3. Choose Network. A dialog box similar to the one shown in Figure 3-24 appears.

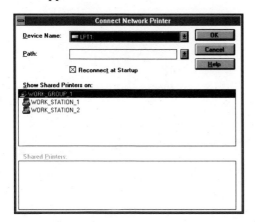

FIGURE 3-24. *The Connect Network Printer dialog box.*

To connect to a network printer using the Connect Network Printer dialog box, follow these steps:

1. Select the local port (LPT1, LPT2, LPT3, and so on) you want to use from the Device Name drop-down list.

2. Specify the network printer to which you want to connect. First select the remote computer whose printer you want to access from the Show Shared Printers On list box. (The list box displays both the workgroup names and the computers in the workgroups.) Then select the printer to which you want to connect from the Shared Printers list box. If you want to connect to a printer you had connected to previously, select the printer from the Path drop-down list.

3. Select the Reconnect At Startup check box to make the connection when Windows starts.

4. Choose OK.

5. If the printer is protected with a password, a dialog box appears that prompts you for the password. Type in the password and choose OK.

Removing a Printer

To remove a printer from the Installed Printers list, follow these steps:

1. Select the name of the printer to be removed from the Installed Printers list.

2. Choose Remove. A dialog box appears asking you to confirm the printer's removal. Choose Yes to remove the printer, or No to cancel the procedure.

Selecting the Default Printer

If your computer has multiple printers installed, you must select one printer as the default printer. Unless you specify otherwise, all print files are sent to the default printer. You can change the default printer at any time. To select a default printer, follow these steps:

1. Select a printer from the Installed Printers list.

2. Choose Set As Default Printer.

SPECIFYING INTERNATIONAL SETTINGS

To specify the date, time, number, and currency formats—as well as the keyboard layout—that Windows is to use, double-click on the Control Panel's International icon. A dialog box similar to the one shown in Figure 3-25 appears.

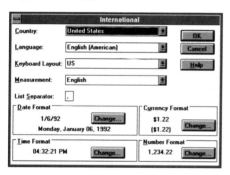

FIGURE 3-25. *The International dialog box.*

The following paragraphs describe the fields in this dialog box. To change the value of one of the first four fields, follow these steps:

1. Select the field, and open its drop-down list.

2. Choose an item from the list.

Country This field controls the country whose formats, measurement system, and list-separator character Windows uses. When you choose a country, Windows changes every field in the dialog box except Language and Keyboard Layout to reflect the default formats used in that country.

Language This field controls the language that Windows-based applications use when sorting lists and converting the case of letters.

Keyboard Layout This field controls the keyboard layout Windows uses. The keyboard layout accommodates special characters for each country's language.

Measurement This field controls the measurement system Windows uses.

List Separator This field controls the symbol used to separate items in a list. To use a different symbol, select the List Separator box and type in the new symbol.

Date Format You can change the format used to display the date within applications that have a date function. For example, you can vary the order *month-day-year* or change the punctuation used to separate the parts of the date. To change the date format, choose Change in the Date Format box. A dialog box similar to the one shown in Figure 3-26 appears.

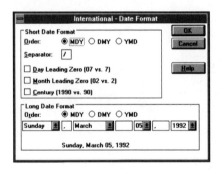

FIGURE 3-26. *The International - Date Format dialog box.*

The Short Date Format displays the date as three numbers representing the month, day, and year. You specify the order and number of digits for each part of the date. The Long Date Format displays the date as a combination of words and numbers. Select the options that suit your needs, and then choose OK.

Time Format You can choose either the 12-hour or the 24-hour format, specifying the separator between the parts and displaying numbers representing the hours before 10 with a leading zero if you want. To change the time format, choose Change in the Time Format box. The International - Time Format dialog box appears. Select the options that suit your needs and choose OK.

Currency Format You can control currency formatting by specifying the symbol used, symbol placement, number of decimal digits, and format of negative values. To control currency formatting, choose Change in the Currency Format box. The International - Currency Format dialog box appears. Select the options that suit your needs and choose OK.

Number Format You can control the way numbers are displayed in Windows and in many Windows-based applications by specifying the thousands separator, the decimal separator, the number of decimal digits, and whether a leading zero is displayed before a decimal value. To make modifications, choose Change in the Number Format box. The International - Number Format dialog box appears. Select the options that suit your needs and choose OK.

SETTING THE COMPUTER'S DATE AND TIME

To change the computer's internal date and time, double-click on the Control Panel's Date/Time icon. A dialog box similar to the one shown in Figure 3-27 appears.

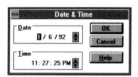

FIGURE 3-27. *The Date & Time dialog box.*

To set your computer's date, follow these steps:

1. Click on the date field you want to change.
2. Type in the new value or click on the Date box's up or down arrow to increase or decrease the value in that field.

To set your computer's time, follow these steps:

1. Click on the time field you want to change.
2. Type in the new value or click on the Time box's up or down arrow to increase or decrease the value in that field.

After you finish setting the date and time, choose OK.

MODIFYING NETWORK SETTINGS

Use the Networks option in the Control Panel window to modify the network settings your computer uses. You can also use this option to set up auditing of network activity and log onto and log off the network. When you double-click on the Networks icon in the Control Panel window, a dialog box similar to the one shown in Figure 3-28 appears.

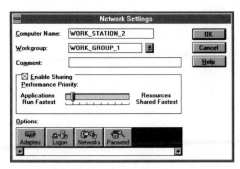

FIGURE 3-28. *The Network Settings dialog box.*

Changing Your Computer Name

You might want to change your computer name so that it's easily recognizable to other users on your network. To do so, type the desired name in the Computer Name text box. The change will not take effect until you log off and then log onto the network again.

Changing Workgroups

Depending on your job responsibilities, you might change from one workgroup to another throughout the day. You might also want to create a new workgroup. To change workgroups, select the desired workgroup name from the Workgroup drop-down list. To create a workgroup, type a unique name in the Workgroup text box.

Adding a Comment to Your Computer Name

When you add a comment, it is displayed next to your computer name when any user views the list of computers on the network. To add a comment, type it in the Comment text box.

Controlling Resource Sharing and Performance Priority

The File Manager lets you share your directories. Likewise, you can use the Print Manager to share printers. The Enable Sharing check box controls whether such network resource sharing is allowed. If, for some reason, you want to temporarily prevent shared resource access, you can do so by deselecting this check box.

Sharing resources can cause your programs to run slower. The Performance Priority bar lets you control whether Windows gives preference to local applications or to shared resources. Using the System Meter program, you can measure the amount of processor time each consumes and decide whether you need to change your performance priority.

Options

The Options field in the Network Settings dialog box includes five buttons that let you modify many network settings.

Changing network adapters

Windows lets you remove or add a network adapter and modify the settings of the installed network adapter. To make these changes, choose the Adapters button. A dialog box similar to the one shown in Figure 3-29 appears.

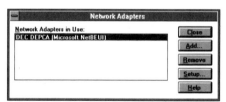

FIGURE 3-29. *The Network Adapters dialog box.*

To delete an adapter, select the adapter's name and choose the Remove button. To add information about an adapter, choose the Add button and select the adapter's name from the list in the dialog box that appears.

To change the settings of your adapter, choose the Setup command and make your changes in the dialog box that appears.

Logging on, logging off, and controlling logon options

Windows lets you log onto or log off the network and control the startup logon options. To perform these tasks, choose the Logon button. The dialog box shown in Figure 3-30 appears.

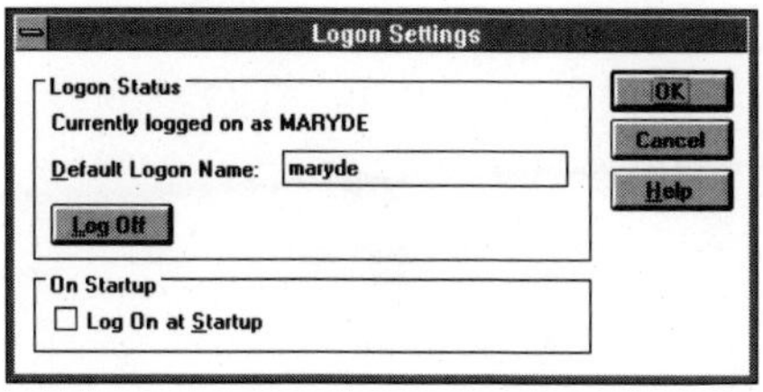

FIGURE 3-30. *The Logon Settings dialog box.*

To log off the network, choose the Log Off button. Windows displays a dialog box warning you that all network connections will be broken and asking if you want to continue. Choose Yes to log off the network. Choose No to cancel the operation.

If you are currently not connected to the network, choose the Log On button. Windows displays the Welcome to Windows for Workgroups dialog box, which prompts you for your name and password. Type in the information and choose OK.

You can also control whether Windows logs onto the network when it first starts. Select the Log On At Startup check box to make Windows log on automatically.

Using other networks

You can use network software such as Novell NetWare or Microsoft LAN Manager concurrently with Windows for Workgroups to access machines that are using the other network software just as if they were using the Windows for Workgroups software. To set up the other network in Windows for Workgroups, choose the Networks button. The dialog box shown in Figure 3-31 on the next page appears.

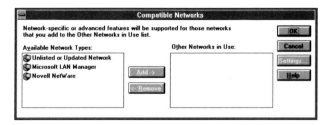

FIGURE 3-31. *The Other Networks dialog box.*

Choose the network you want to set up from the Available Network Types list box and choose Add. If you want to change the network's settings, choose Add and modify the settings in the dialog box that appears. When you are finished, choose OK.

Changing your network password

To change the password you use to log onto the network, follow these steps:

1. Choose the Password button. The dialog box shown in Figure 3-32 appears.

FIGURE 3-32. *The Change Logon Password dialog box.*

2. Type your old password in the Old Password text box.

3. Type your new password in the New Password text box.

4. Retype your new password in the Confirm New Password text box.

5. Choose OK.

USING THE MIDI MAPPER

MIDI stands for Musical Instrument Digital Interface. It allows several devices, instruments, and computers to send messages to and receive messages from each other for the purpose of creating music, sound, or lighting.

You can use the Control Panel's MIDI Mapper option to select a MIDI setup for a sound device; create a new setup; or edit existing key maps, patch maps, and channel mappings. Windows supplies MIDI setups for the sound devices it supports. Unless you connect a synthesizer to the MIDI output port of your computer, you do not need to use the MIDI Mapper to create or edit a MIDI setup. For more information about the MIDI Mapper, see *Windows for Workgroups Companion* (Microsoft Press, 1992).

ASSIGNING SOUNDS TO SYSTEM EVENTS

By default, Windows beeps when you try to do something you are not allowed to do. (For example, you hear a beep when you try to move the cursor past the end of a Write document.) The Control Panel Sound option lets you turn the warning beep on and off. In addition, if you have installed a sound card and a sound device driver, you can assign various sounds to different system events. When you double-click on the Sound icon, a dialog box similar to the one shown in Figure 3-33 appears. (If you haven't installed a sound card, items in the Events and Files list boxes appear dimmed and are not selectable.)

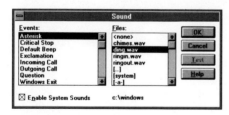

FIGURE 3-33. *The Sound dialog box.*

To enable system sounds, select the Enable System Sounds check box. To disable system sounds, deselect the check box.

To assign a sound to a specific system event, follow these steps:

1. Select the event to which you want to assign the sound from the Events list box.

2. Select the sound you want to assign from the Files list box. To hear the sound, choose Test.

To remove a sound from an event, follow these steps:

1. Select the event from which you want to remove the sound from the Files list box.

2. Select the <none> option from the Files list box. This option restores the normal PC beep.

3. Choose OK.

USING 386 ENHANCED MODE OPTIONS

If you own a computer that uses an 80386SX, 80386, i486SX, i486, or compatible microprocessor, Windows runs in 386 enhanced mode. 386 enhanced mode lets one or more applications not designed for Windows run at the same time as Windows-based applications.

Handling Device Contention

When Windows-based applications and MS-DOS–based applications are running simultaneously, they sometimes try to use a device, such as a printer or modem, at the same time. (Such jockeying for resources is called *device contention.*) To specify how Windows is to handle this situation, follow these steps:

1. Double-click on the 386 Enhanced icon in the Control Panel window. A dialog box similar to the one shown in Figure 3-34 appears.

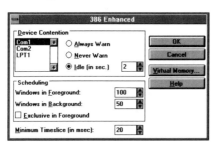

FIGURE 3-34. *The 386 Enhanced dialog box.*

2. Select the device from the Device Contention list.

3. Select the option button that best suits your needs. The following table describes the options:

Windows Action	Result
Always Warn	Windows displays a warning dialog box each time an application tries to use a device already in use. The dialog box asks you to choose the application that should gain control of the device.

(continued)

continued

Windows Action	Result
Never Warn	Windows lets any application use the device at any time; you receive no warning. This might result in two applications trying to use the device at the same time, with undesirable results.
Idle	Specifies the number of seconds (from 1 through 999) a device is to be idle before a second application can use it. If a second application tries to use the device before the idle period is complete, a warning message appears.

386 Enhanced Mode Scheduling Options

When multiple applications are running simultaneously, Windows runs one application for awhile and then switches to the next application and runs it for a certain amount of time, repeating the process for each application. You can dictate how much time Windows spends on its applications when the active window (called the foreground application) is a Windows-based application. You can also specify how much time Windows spends on applications for Windows when a non-Windows (that is, an MS-DOS–based) application is active (in the foreground) and all the Windows applications are running in the background. To do so, follow these steps:

1. Double-click on the 386 Enhanced icon in the Control Panel window. A dialog box similar to the one previously shown in Figure 3-34 appears.

2. Select the Windows In Foreground text box, and enter a number from 1 through 10,000. Use this field to specify how much time Windows spends running a Windows-based application when it is in the foreground.

3. Select the Windows In Background text box, and enter a number from 1 through 10,000. This number controls how much time Windows spends running Windows-based applications when they are in the background and an MS-DOS–based application is in the foreground.

4. Select Exclusive In Foreground to specify that Windows-based applications get 100 percent of the computer's processing time whenever a Windows-based application is active. (MS-DOS–based applications in the background are suspended.)

5. Select the Minimum Timeslice text box, and enter a number from 1 through 1000. This is the number of milliseconds (thousandths of a second) that Windows spends executing each application.

Creating Windows Swap Files

When Windows gets low on memory, it temporarily copies information to a file on your hard disk. When the information is needed again, Windows copies it back from the file into memory. This process of moving information from memory to a file on the hard disk and back to memory again is called *swapping*. The file to which information is copied is called a *swap file*.

Windows supports two types of swap files: *temporary* and *permanent*. A permanent swap file is often a better choice because Windows can access a permanent swap file more quickly. A permanent swap file does, however, take up hard disk space—even when Windows is not in use. If you use Windows extensively in 386 enhanced mode, the permanent swap file provides the best performance. If you don't use Windows extensively, you might want to sacrifice performance for available hard disk space and use a temporary swap file instead.

To create a swap file, follow these steps:

1. Choose Virtual Memory in the 386 Enhanced dialog box. A dialog box similar to the one shown in Figure 3-35 appears.

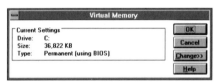

FIGURE 3-35. *The Virtual Memory dialog box.*

2. If you're satisfied with your existing swap file, choose Cancel; otherwise, choose Change. The Virtual Memory dialog box changes to resemble Figure 3-36.

```
┌─────────── Virtual Memory ────────────┐
│ ┌Current Settings──────────┐  ┌──────┐│
│ │ Drive:   C:              │  │  OK  ││
│ │ Size:    36,822 KB       │  ├──────┤│
│ │ Type:    Permanent (using BIOS)│ │Cancel││
│ │                          │  ├──────┤│
│ │                          │  │Change>>││
│ │                          │  ├──────┤│
│ │                          │  │ Help ││
│ │                          │  └──────┘│
│ └──────────────────────────┘          │
│ ┌New Settings──────────────────────┐  │
│ │ Drive:  [▤ c: [my_drive]    ] ▲▼ │  │
│ │ Type:   [Permanent          ] ▲▼ │  │
│ │                                  │  │
│ │ Space Available:      93,890 KB  │  │
│ │ Maximum Size:         42,896 KB  │  │
│ │ Recommended Size:     19,696 KB  │  │
│ │                                  │  │
│ │ New Size:            [19696] KB  │  │
│ └──────────────────────────────────┘  │
│ ☐ Use 32-Bit Disk Access              │
└────────────────────────────────────────┘
```

FIGURE 3-36. *The expanded Virtual Memory dialog box.*

3. Choose the drive on which the swap file is to reside from the Drives drop-down list.

4. Choose the swap file's type from the Type drop-down list.

5. Type the size of the swap file in the New Size text box.

6. If your hard disk controller can handle 32-bit access, you can choose whether to use it. Select the Use 32-Bit Disk Access check box to turn on 32-bit access. This type of access decreases the amount of time needed for accesssing the disk and thus speeds up swap file activities.

7. Choose OK. If you've modified any fields, Windows asks you whether you want to make changes to your virtual memory settings. Choose Yes to make the changes.

8. Windows tells you that you need to restart Windows so that the changes you made can take effect. Choose Restart Windows to immediately restart Windows, or choose Continue to continue the current session. (The changes you made take effect the next time you start Windows.)

MANAGING DEVICE DRIVERS

Device drivers allow hardware devices such as sound cards and video players to communicate with Windows. The Drivers option in the Control Panel window lets you install, remove, and configure device drivers. When you double-click on the Drivers icon, a dialog box similar to the one shown in Figure 3-37 appears.

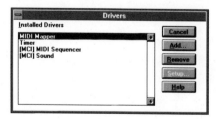

FIGURE 3-37. *The Drivers dialog box.*

Adding a Device Driver

To add a device driver, follow these steps:

1. Select Add. The Add dialog box, similar to the one shown in Figure 3-38 on the following page, appears.

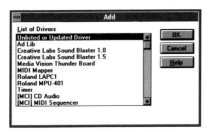

FIGURE 3-38. *The Add dialog box.*

2. Select the desired driver from the List Of Drivers list box and choose OK. (If the device driver you want is not listed, select Unlisted Or Updated Driver.) A dialog box that prompts you to insert a disk appears. Insert the requested disk into the disk drive and choose OK. (You can type a different drive and path in the text box if necessary.)

3. After Windows installs the device driver, it displays a dialog box for setting up the device. Figure 3-39 shows the setup dialog box for a Sound Blaster. Select the port and interrupt that the device uses, and then choose OK.

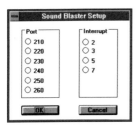

FIGURE 3-39. *The Sound Blaster Setup dialog box.*

4. You need to restart Windows before the device driver can take effect. Windows displays a dialog box asking whether you want to restart Windows now. Remove the disk from the disk drive and choose Restart Now.

Removing a Device Driver

If Windows has a device driver installed that you don't use, you can remove the device driver to free up memory for other uses. To remove a device driver, follow these steps:

1. Select the device driver you want to remove from the Installed Drivers list box in the Drivers dialog box. Choose Remove.

2. Windows displays a dialog box asking you to confirm the deletion. Choose Yes.

3. You need to restart Windows before the device driver can be removed. Windows displays a dialog box asking whether you want to restart Windows now. Choose Restart Now.

Reconfiguring a Device Driver

As you add hardware to your computer, you might find that one device driver conflicts with another. To solve this problem, configure one of the device drivers to use a different port or interrupt. To configure a device driver, follow these steps:

1. Select the device driver to be configured from the Installed Drivers list box in the Drivers dialog box. Choose Setup.

2. Windows displays the driver's setup dialog box, an example of which is shown in Figure 3-39. Select the port and interrupt that the device uses, and then choose OK.

PART IV

Desktop Accessories

Windows provides a powerful collection of *desktop accessories,* which are productivity tools designed to help you perform a variety of tasks directly from the Windows desktop:

Write	Allows you to perform word processing
Paintbrush	Allows you to create figures and drawings
Terminal	Permits telecommunications
Notepad	Allows you to edit ASCII text files
Recorder	Records macros
Cardfile	Lists information
Calculator	Performs business and statistical calculations
Clock	Keeps track of the time
Object Packager	Allows you to place in a file an icon that represents an embedded or linked object
Character Map	Lets you insert special characters and symbols into a document
Media Player	Allows you to control multimedia hardware such as a sound card or a CD-ROM drive
Sound Recorder	Lets you play, record, and edit sound files
Chat	Lets two users have an interactive, typed conversation over the network
WinMeter	Displays a graph of your system utilization, contrasting resource use by local programs with use by remote programs
Net Watcher	Lets you view and control other users' connections to your computer

These programs are found in the Accessories group window, shown in Figure 4-1.

This section provides an overview of each desktop accessory program. First, however, this section presents two sets of actions available to most Windows desktop accessories: Page Setup options and Printer options.

FIGURE 4-1. *The Accessories group window.*

PAGE SETUP OPTIONS

Several Windows accessories—including Paintbrush, Notepad, and Cardfile—allow you to set the margins and add formatted headers and footers to your printouts.

Setting Margins

To set the margins of your printouts, follow these steps:

1. Choose Page Setup from the application's File menu. The Page Setup dialog box, similar to the one shown in Figure 4-2, appears.

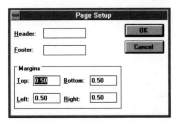

FIGURE 4-2. *The Page Setup dialog box.*

2. In the Margins area, type the measurements you want for your margins.

3. Choose OK.

Inserting Headers and Footers

To insert a header or a footer into your printouts, follow these steps:

1. Choose Page Setup from the application's File menu. The Page Setup dialog box, similar to the one shown in Figure 4-2, appears.

2. Type the header or footer text into the Header or Footer text box. The table below includes the character codes used to format the header or footer.

Character Code	Function
&d	Inserts the current date
&p	Inserts the current page number
&f	Inserts the current filename
&l	Aligns the text following the code at the left margin
&r	Aligns the text following the code at the right margin
&c	Centers the text following the code
&t	Inserts the current time

3. Choose OK.

CHANGING PRINTERS AND PRINTER OPTIONS

Many Windows accessories allow you to set up a printer before printing. This includes selecting a printer (useful if you've installed several printers) and changing a printer's options. To change printers or printer options, follow these steps:

1. Choose Print Setup from the File menu. A dialog box similar to the one shown in Figure 4-3 appears.

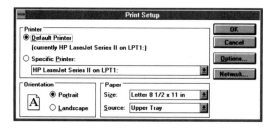

FIGURE 4-3. *The Print Setup dialog box.*

2. Select a printer from the Specific Printer drop-down list, if necessary. (If you want to connect to a new network printer, click on the Network button.)

3. Select the Orientation and Paper specifications as necessary.

4. To set options specific to your printer, choose Options. A dialog box containing printer setup options appears.

5. Select printer options as necessary. The options in this dialog box vary depending on the printer you've installed. See your printer's manual for information about your printer's options, or press F1 for help.

6. Choose OK in the Print Setup dialog box.

REMOTE RESOURCES AND ACCESSORIES

Windows enables you to use remote resources, such as shared directories on machines in your workgroup, network printers, and shared local printers. You can use all of these resources within the Windows accessories. For example, using Write, you could open or save a file on a remote computer that has a shared directory, or you could print a document on a shared printer.

WRITE

Write is a word processing application that lets you create and edit professional-quality letters and reports. Beyond performing the normal editing tasks of cutting and pasting text, Write lets you align paragraphs, use different character fonts, and even integrate graphics images you create with Paintbrush.

Starting Write

To start Write, double-click on Write's icon in the Accessories group window. A window appears, similar to the one shown in Figure 4-4.

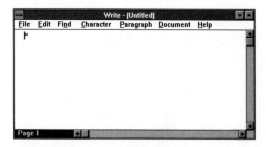

FIGURE 4-4. *A new Write window.*

Opening, Creating, and Saving Documents

To open an existing document, choose Open from Write's File menu. The Open dialog box appears. Select the drive and directory where the file is stored in the Drives drop-down list and the Directories list box, and type the name of the file in the File Name text box. Choose OK.

To create a new document, choose New from the File menu. If you've made any changes to the current document, Write first asks whether you want to save the changes to the current document.

After you complete the document, you need to save it to a file on disk. To do so, choose Save As from Write's File menu. The Save As dialog box appears. Select the drive and directory on which the file is to be saved in the Drives drop-down list and the Directories list box, and then type a filename in the File Name text box. Then choose OK.

Write's File Menu

The following table describes the commands on Write's File menu.

Command	Function
New	Creates a new document, first asking whether you want to save any changes to the current document
Open	Lets you load an existing document
Save	Saves a document
Save As	Saves a document with a new name
Print	Prints the document
Print Setup	Lets you select a printer and change its options
Repaginate	Repaginates a document
Exit	Closes the Write window

Moving Through Your Document

To move through a document, use the arrow, PgUp, PgDn, Home, and End keys, or the vertical and horizontal scroll bars if you're using a mouse.

The following table lists keyboard combinations that help you move around the window:

Keyboard Combination	Cursor Movement
Home	Moves the cursor to the start of the current line
End	Moves the cursor to the end of the current line
Ctrl+Home	Moves the cursor to the start of the document

(continued)

continued

Keyboard Combination	Cursor Movement
Ctrl+End	Moves the cursor to the end of the document
PgUp	Moves the cursor up one page
PgDn	Moves the cursor down one page
Ctrl+PgUp	Moves the cursor to the top of the page
Ctrl+PgDn	Moves the cursor to the bottom of the page
Ctrl+right arrow	Moves the cursor right one word
Ctrl+left arrow	Moves the cursor left one word
Goto+right arrow*	Moves the cursor to the next sentence
Goto+left arrow*	Moves the cursor to the previous sentence
Goto+down arrow*	Moves the cursor to the next paragraph
Goto+up arrow*	Moves the cursor to the previous paragraph
Goto+PgDn*	Moves the cursor to the next page, according to the last repagination
Goto+PgUp*	Moves the cursor to the previous page, according to the last repagination

*Goto represents the numeric keypad 5 key.

Editing Your Document

Write lets you move, copy, or delete sections of your document. To use Write's edit menu, you must first select the text you want to manipulate. To do so with the mouse, position the mouse pointer over the start of the text, hold down the mouse button, and then drag the mouse pointer to the last of the text you want to select. Then release the mouse button.

With the keyboard, move the cursor to the beginning of the text, hold down the Shift key, and then use the arrow keys to move the cursor to the end of the text you want to select. Then release the Shift key.

Moving text

To move text from one location to another, first select the text to move, and choose Cut from the Edit menu. Then move the cursor to the location in the document where you want to place the text, and choose Paste from the Edit menu.

Copying text

To copy text from one location to another, first select the text to copy, and choose Copy from the Edit menu. Then move the cursor to the location in the document to which you want to copy the text. Choose Paste from the Edit menu. Repeat this step at each location to which you want to copy the text.

Deleting text

To delete text, simply select the text, and choose Cut from the Edit menu.

Adding graphics

Write lets you paste graphics images into a document from the Clipboard. To paste a graphics image you have created using Paintbrush (such as a logo) into your Write document, follow these steps:

1. Within Paintbrush, use the Scissors tool or the Pick tool to select the image and then choose Copy from the Edit menu to place the image on the Clipboard. (See ''Paintbrush,'' later in this section.)

2. Start Write, and open the document in which the image is to be placed.

3. Move to the location in the document where you want the image to appear. Choose Paste from the Edit menu.

Sizing an image After you place the image in the document, you can re-size it to suit your needs. To resize an image, follow these steps:

1. Select the image by clicking on it.

2. Choose Size Picture from the Edit menu. A box appears around the image, and the mouse pointer changes to a box-within-a-box shape.

3. Use the mouse or the arrow keys to resize the box surrounding the image. When the box is the correct size, click the mouse or press Enter. The image is redrawn at the new size.

Positioning an image After you place the image in the document, you can move it to suit your needs. To move an image, follow these steps:

1. Select the image by clicking on it.

2. Choose Move Picture from the Edit menu. A box appears around the image, and the mouse pointer changes to a box-within-a-box shape.

3. Use the mouse or the arrow keys to move the box surrounding the image. When the box is positioned properly, click the mouse or press Enter. The image is redrawn at the new location.

Using Embedded Objects

Write's Edit menu lets you place an embedded object or a link to an object within your document. For more information on links and embedded objects, refer to the section titled ''Object Packager,'' on page 201.

Using the Find Menu

The Find menu provides several ways of searching for text in a document.

Searching for a word or a phrase

To search your document for a string of text, follow these steps:

1. Choose Find from Write's Find menu. A dialog box appears, similar to the one shown in Figure 4-5.

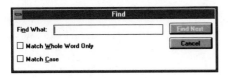

FIGURE 4-5. *The Find dialog box.*

2. Type the text you are searching for in the Find What text box.

3. Select Match Whole Word Only if you want Write to distinguish the text string from longer words that might contain the text string (for example, if you want Write to find the word *book* but ignore the word *bookmark*).

4. Select Match Case if you want Write to match uppercase and lowercase letters exactly (for example, if you want Write to find *Book* but not *book*).

5. Choose Find Next. If Write finds the text in the document, it displays the part of the document containing the text and highlights the text; otherwise, it displays a dialog box telling you it didn't find the text.

6. To search for another occurrence of the text, choose Find Next; otherwise, choose Cancel.

Changing a word or a phrase

Write lets you quickly search for and change each occurrence of a word or a phrase throughout your document. To change a word or a phrase, follow these steps:

1. Move to the location in the document where you want the changes to begin.

2. Choose Replace from the Find menu. A dialog box appears, similar to the one shown in Figure 4-6 on the following page.

FIGURE 4-6. *The Replace dialog box.*

3. In the Find What text box, type the word or phrase you want to change, but do *not* press Enter. In the Replace With field, type the desired replacement word or phrase, but do *not* press Enter.

4. Select Match Whole Word Only if you want Write to distinguish the Find What text from longer words that might contain the text (for example, if you want Write to find the word *book* but ignore the word *bookmark*).

5. Select Match Case if you want Write to match uppercase and lowercase letters exactly (for example, if you want Write to find *Book* but not *book*).

6. Choose the button that best suits your needs:

Find Button	Result
Find Next	Finds the next match without changing the current one
Replace	Changes the current match and finds the next one
Replace All	Changes all matching text, starting from the beginning of the document
Replace Selection	Changes all occurrences of the Find What text in the selected portion of the document
Close	Cancels the replace operation

Moving to a specific page

To move to a specific page in the document, follow these steps:

1. Choose Go To Page from the Find menu. A dialog box appears, similar to the one shown in Figure 4-7.

FIGURE 4-7. *The Go To dialog box.*

2. Type in the number of the page to which you'd like to move, and then choose OK.

Changing Character Fonts

Write provides several character fonts for use in your Write documents. Write gives you two ways to select and use fonts. You can select a specific font, and then type. (The text you type appears in the new font.) Or you can change any existing text to a new font. To do so, follow these steps:

1. Select the desired text.

2. Choose Fonts from the Character menu. A dialog box appears, similar to the one shown in Figure 4-8.

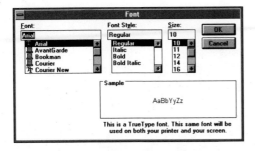

FIGURE 4-8. *The Font dialog box.*

3. Select a font from the Font list box, a font style from the Font Style list box, and a size from the Size list box, and then choose OK.

As you select different font, style, and size combinations, Write displays corresponding sample text in the Sample box.

Using the Character Menu

Write's Character menu lets you select text attributes such as bold, underlined, or italic. Reduce Font and Enlarge Font incrementally decrease or increase a font size. For best results, use these commands with the TrueType fonts that come with Windows.

Using the Paragraph Menu

Write automatically wraps text when it reaches the end of a line. The only time you need to press Enter is to start a new paragraph. Write's Paragraph menu lets you specify paragraph alignment, line spacing within paragraphs, and paragraph indentation. The following table briefly describes the formatting commands available on the Paragraph menu:

Commands	Function
Left	Aligns text along the left margin only
Centered	Centers each line of text between the left and right margins
Right	Aligns text along the right margin only
Justified	Aligns text along the left and right margins
Single Space	Single-spaces a paragraph
1½ Space	Uses 1½ spaces between lines in a paragraph
Double Space	Double-spaces a paragraph
Indents	Lets you set paragraph indents

NOTE: *If you have a mouse, you can set these paragraph values with the Ruler. See "Using the Document Ruler," later in this section.*

Changing paragraph alignment

To change a paragraph's alignment, first place the cursor within the paragraph to be aligned, and then select the desired alignment from the Paragraph menu.

Changing paragraph spacing

Write lets you single-space, double-space, or triple-space the lines of text in a paragraph. To change a paragraph's line spacing, first place the cursor within the desired paragraph, and then select the desired line spacing from the Paragraph menu.

Changing paragraph indentation

Write lets you indent a paragraph from the left and right margins. The first line can be indented separately to make it stand out. To indent a paragraph, follow these steps:

1. Place the cursor within the paragraph you want to change.

2. Choose Indents from the Paragraph menu. A dialog box appears, similar to the one shown in Figure 4-9.

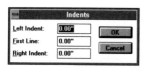

FIGURE 4-9. *The Indents dialog box.*

3. Type in the indentations you want, and then choose OK.

Using the Document Menu

Write's Document menu lets you control elements that affect your entire document.

Adding a header or a footer

A *header* is text—such as a title, your name, or a page number—that appears at the top of each page throughout your document. Likewise, a *footer* is text that appears at the bottom of each page. To add a header or a footer to your document, follow these steps:

1. Choose Header or Footer from Write's Document menu. A window appears, in which you type the text for the header or footer, along with a dialog box that lets you provide certain information about the text, as shown in Figure 4-10.

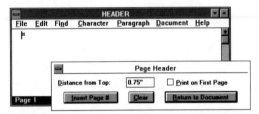

FIGURE 4-10. *The Header window and the Page Header dialog box.*

2. Type the text for the header or footer in the Header window. When you're satisfied with the text, move to the Page Header dialog box by clicking in it.

3. In the Distance From Top text box (if you're creating a footer, the text box is Distance From Bottom), specify a value—in inches—that dictates how far the header or footer falls from the top (header) or bottom (footer) of the page.

4. Select the Print On First Page check box if you want your header or footer to appear on the first page.

5. Choose Insert Page # if you want page numbers to accompany your header or footer.

6. If you're happy with your choices, choose Return To Document. If you'd like to revise your header or footer, return to the Header window by clicking in it, and edit your header or footer text. Or, if you want to start from scratch, simply choose Clear in the Page Header dialog box to erase the header or footer text, and return to the Header window. Begin again at step 2, above.

Setting tab stops

By default, Write sets tab stops at every half inch. You can set up to 12 tab stops of your own. To do so, follow these steps.

NOTE: *If you are using a mouse, you can set tabs with the document ruler. See "Using the Document Ruler," later in this section.*

1. Choose Tabs from Write's Document menu. A dialog box similar to the one shown in Figure 4-11 appears.

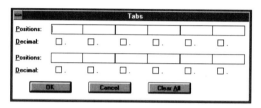

FIGURE 4-11. *The Tabs dialog box.*

2. Select an empty Positions text box.

3. Type in the tab stop's distance from the left margin in inches. Include an inchmark (") after the number.

4. Select the corresponding Decimal check box if you want to align decimal points in a column of numbers.

5. After you finish setting tab stops, choose OK.

Deleting a tab stop

To delete a tab stop, follow these steps:

1. Choose Tabs from the Document menu.

2. Select the Positions text box for the tab stop you want to remove.

3. Use the Backspace key to delete the measurement.

4. After you finish deleting tab stops, choose OK.

Using the Document Ruler

The *document ruler* is a ruler and a group of icons that Write displays below its menu bar to help you view and control tab stops, margins, and indentation, as shown in Figure 4-12.

To toggle the ruler on or off, choose Ruler On or Ruler Off from the Document menu.

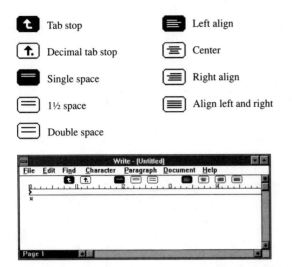

🔼 Tab stop		▬ Left align
🔼 Decimal tab stop		☰ Center
▬ Single space		☰ Right align
☰ 1½ space		☰ Align left and right
☰ Double space		

FIGURE 4-12. *The document ruler displays your screen measurements.*

Setting tab stops with the document ruler

To set tab stops with the document ruler, follow these steps:

1. Click on the icon for the type of tab stop you want (normal or decimal).

2. Click on the ruler at the location where you want the tab stop to appear.

Changing and removing tab stops with the document ruler

To change a tab stop using the document ruler, drag the tab stop to its new location. To remove a tab stop, drag it off the document ruler.

Setting paragraph line spacing with the document ruler

To set paragraph line spacing with the document ruler, first click anywhere within the paragraph you want to format, and then click on the icon for the type of line spacing you want.

Setting paragraph alignment with the document ruler

To set paragraph alignment with the document ruler, first click anywhere within the paragraph you want to format, and then click on the icon for the type of alignment you want.

Setting the Page Layout

To change Write's default page numbering, margin widths, or measurement settings, use the following steps.

1. Choose Page Layout from Write's Document menu. The Page Layout dialog box appears.

2. Type the starting page number in the Start Page Numbers At text box in the Page Layout dialog box.

3. Type the measurements you want for your margins in the Margins text boxes in the Page Layout dialog box.

4. Select the system of measurement you prefer using the Measurements option buttons in the Page Layout dialog box.

5. Choose OK.

PAINTBRUSH

Paintbrush lets you create your own graphics images or enhance graphics images created by a scanner or a screen-capture program.

NOTE: *If you try to use Paintbrush without a mouse, you'll quickly become frustrated. Accordingly, this section focuses on mouse operations. For more information on keyboard combinations—and for a detailed description of the Paintbrush program—see* Windows for Workgroups Companion *by Russell Borland (Microsoft Press, 1992).*

Starting Paintbrush

To start Paintbrush, double-click on the Paintbrush icon in the Accessories group window. A window appears, similar to the one shown in Figure 4-13.

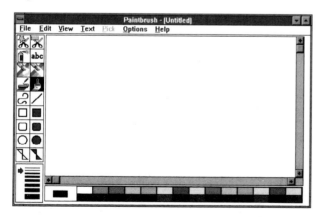

FIGURE 4-13. *A new Paintbrush window.*

Using the File Menu

The following table describes the commands available on Paintbrush's File menu:

Command	Function
New	Creates a new image, first prompting you to either save or discard any changes to the current image
Open	Lets you load an existing image
Save	Saves the current image
Save As	Lets you save the current image with a new name
Page Setup	Lets you define printer margins as well as insert a header and a footer for each page
Print	Prints the current image
Printer Setup	Lets you select a printer and change its options
Exit	Closes the Paintbrush window

Paintbrush provides a collection of drawing tools, described below:

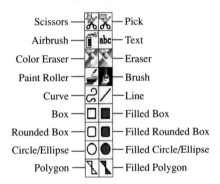

Tool	Function
Scissors	Selects a free-form portion of the image to move, copy, or delete
Pick	Selects a rectangular portion of the image to move, copy, or delete
Airbrush	Spray-paints the image with the foreground color
Text	Places text in the image
Color Eraser	Changes portions of the foreground color to the background color, or changes every occurrence of one color to another
Eraser	Changes portions of the drawing to the background color
Paint Roller	Fills an area with the foreground color

(continued)

continued

Tool	Function
Brush	Paints using the foreground color
Curve	Draws a smooth curved line
Line	Draws a straight line
Box	Draws an unfilled rectangle
Filled Box	Draws a rectangle filled with the foreground color
Rounded Box	Draws an unfilled rectangle with rounded corners
Filled Rounded Box	Draws a rectangle with rounded edges, filled with the foreground color
Circle/Ellipse	Draws an unfilled ellipse
Filled Circle/Ellipse	Draws an ellipse filled with the foreground color
Polygon	Draws an unfilled irregular shape
Filled Polygon	Draws an irregular shape filled with the foreground color

Selecting a Tool

To select a tool, simply click on the tool.

Selecting Line Thickness

Below the Paintbrush tool set are eight horizontal lines of varying thickness. You use these lines to define the thickness Paintbrush uses to draw or erase lines and shapes. To change the thickness, simply click on the line with the desired thickness.

Selecting Colors

To the right of the line-size box is the color palette, along with the foreground and background color indicator. To select a foreground color, simply click (using the left mouse button) on the desired color. To select a background color, click (using the right mouse button) on the color you want.

NOTE: *If you have swapped the functions of the mouse buttons, as described in Part III, you'll use the right button to select the foreground color and the left button to select the background color.*

Using the Paintbrush Tools

The following sections briefly describe the use of each Paintbrush tool.

Working with the Scissors tool

The Scissors tool lets you select an irregularly shaped area. (After creating this "cutout," you can perform a variety of operations on it. See "Fun with Cutouts," later in this section.)

To use the Scissors tool, follow these steps:

1. Select the Scissors tool. The mouse pointer changes to a pair of cross hairs.

2. Place the mouse pointer on the starting point of the area to select.

3. Hold down the mouse button, and then draw around the area you want to select. After you completely encircle the area, release the mouse button.

Working with the Pick tool

The Pick tool provides a convenient way to cut out a rectangular area. (After creating such a "cutout," you can perform a variety of operations on it. See "Fun with Cutouts," later in this section.)

To use the Pick tool, follow these steps:

1. Select the Pick tool. The mouse pointer changes to a pair of cross hairs.

2. Place the mouse pointer at the upper left corner of the rectangular area you want to select.

3. Hold down the mouse button, and then move the mouse pointer to create a rectangular border around the desired area. Then release the mouse button.

Working with a Paintbrush Image

The following tips should prove helpful as you begin to create and work with Paintbrush images:

■ If your image is larger than the canvas area, use the horizontal and vertical scroll bars to view different parts of the image.

■ Choose Zoom In from the View menu to temporarily magnify a portion of the image to allow detailed editing. (While you're zoomed in, you edit pixel by pixel with each click of the mouse.) After you finish with the detailed editing, choose Zoom Out from the View menu to restore the image to its normal size.

Copying a Paintbrush image to the Clipboard

To copy a Paintbrush image to the Clipboard, use either the Pick or the Scissors tool to select the image, and then choose Copy from the Edit menu. The image can then be pasted from the Clipboard into another application.

Working with the Airbrush

The Airbrush tool works like a can of spray paint, letting you shade areas. By selecting different line sizes and colors, you can change the Airbrush tool's effect.

To use the Airbrush tool, follow these steps:

1. Select the Airbrush tool. The mouse pointer changes to a pair of cross hairs.

2. Select a foreground color.

3. Press the mouse button to airbrush an area. Hold down the mouse button, and drag the mouse to airbrush a large area. Release the mouse button to shut the Airbrush off. By keeping the Airbrush in one area, you can concentrate the "paint."

Fun with Cutouts

Cutouts can be treated in a variety of ways. The following table provides a simple description of the operations available on the Edit and Pick menus. Experiment! Or, for further information, see *Windows for Workgroups Companion.*

Operation	Description
Cut	Removes the cutout from the window and places it on the Clipboard
Copy	Places a copy of the cutout on the Clipboard
Paste	Pastes a copy of the Clipboard into the window
Flip Horizontal	Flips the cutout from side to side
Flip Vertical	Flips the cutout from top to bottom
Inverse	Inverts the cutout's colors to their complementary colors
Shrink + Grow	Allows you to copy and size a cutout
Tilt	Allows you to copy and skew a cutout
Clear	Changes the area within the original cutout to the background color when you use Shrink + Grow or Tilt

Adding text to an image

Many images you create will need labels, titles, or other text. The Text tool lets you add text to an image. Depending on your image, you will want to select an appropriate font, font size, and text attribute such as bold, italic, or underline. The commands on the Text menu let you do just that.

To add text to your image, follow these steps:

1. Select the Text tool. The mouse pointer changes to an I-beam.

2. Select as the foreground color the color you'd like the text to be.

3. Select Fonts from the Text menu. A dialog box similar to the one shown in Figure 4-14 appears.

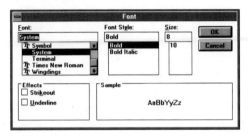

FIGURE 4-14. *The Font dialog box.*

4. Select a font from the Font list box.

5. Select a font style from the Font Style list box.

6. Select a font size from the Size list box.

7. Click on OK to close the Font dialog box.

8. Click on the location where you'd like the text to appear. Type in the desired text.

Erasing areas

Paintbrush's Color Eraser tool and Eraser tool let you erase areas of the image. The Eraser tool erases every color, replacing them with the background color. The Color Eraser, however, erases only text or graphics of the selected foreground color, replacing it with the background color. The selected line size affects how much area the eraser removes at one time. A thick line erases more area, whereas a thin line gives you finer control.

To erase an area, follow these steps:

1. Select either the Color Eraser tool or the Eraser tool. The mouse pointer changes to a square. (If you choose the Color Eraser, a pair of cross hairs will be displayed inside the square.)

2. Select the foreground and background colors.

3. Move the mouse pointer to the area you want to erase.

4. Hold down the mouse button, and then drag the mouse to erase the area.

5. After you finish erasing, release the mouse button.

Changing all of one color to another
To quickly change all of one color to another, follow these steps:

1. Select as the foreground color the color you want to change.

2. Select as the new color the background color.

3. Double-click on the Color Eraser tool.

Using the Paint Roller tool
The Paint Roller tool lets you fill a bordered area with the foreground color. If the border has an opening, the color leaks through the border, filling areas outside the border.

To use the Paint Roller, follow these steps:

1. Select the Paint Roller tool. The mouse pointer changes to a paint roller.

2. Select the desired color for the foreground.

3. Move the mouse pointer into the area you'd like to fill, and press the mouse button.

Using the Brush tool
The Brush tool lets you draw using the foreground color and line thickness. To use the Brush tool, follow these steps:

1. Select the Brush tool. The mouse pointer changes to a square.

2. Select the color you want for the foreground.

3. Select the desired line thickness. The size of the mouse pointer changes to reflect your choice.

4. Move the mouse pointer to the desired location. Hold down the mouse button, and move the mouse to draw.

5. After you finish drawing, release the mouse button.

Drawing lines
The Curve tool and the Line tool let you draw curved and straight lines. To draw a curved line, follow these steps:

1. Select the Curve tool. The mouse pointer changes to a pair of cross hairs.

2. Select the color you want for the foreground.

3. Select the desired line thickness.

4. Click where you want the line to begin, and drag the mouse to the line's ending point to create the desired length. Then release the mouse button.

5. Next hold down the mouse button and drag. The line curves to follow the mouse pointer. When the line has the desired shape, release the mouse button. If you're satisfied with the shape, click on the second endpoint to finalize the curve. If you want to add a second curve to the line, click and drag again.

To create a straight line, follow these steps:

1. Select the Line tool. The mouse pointer changes to a pair of cross hairs.

2. Select the color you want for the foreground.

3. Select the desired line thickness.

4. Click where you want the line to begin, and drag the mouse to create the desired shape. Then release the mouse button.

Drawing boxes

Paintbrush lets you draw four types of boxes: empty boxes, empty boxes with rounded corners, filled boxes, and filled boxes with rounded corners. (The border of a filled box is drawn with the background color and then filled with the foreground color.)

To draw a box, follow these steps:

1. Select the desired box tool. The cursor changes to a pair of cross hairs.

2. Select the desired foreground color. For a filled rectangle, also select a background color.

3. Select the desired line thickness.

4. Move the mouse pointer to the location where you want the box to appear. Drag the mouse to create the desired shape, and then release the mouse button. To draw a perfect square, press the Shift key before releasing the mouse button.

Creating circles and ellipses

Paintbrush lets you create empty or filled circles and ellipses. An *ellipse* is simply an elongated circle. (The border of a filled circle or ellipse is drawn with the background color and then filled with the foreground color.)

To draw a circle or an ellipse, follow these steps:

1. Select the desired circle/ellipse tool. The cursor changes to a pair of cross hairs.

2. Select the desired foreground color. For a filled circle or ellipse, also select a background color.

3. Select the desired line thickness.

4. Move the mouse pointer to the location where you want the circle or ellipse to appear. Drag the mouse to create the desired shape, and then release the mouse button. (You'll have the tendency to create an ellipse. If you want to ensure that you draw a true circle, press the Shift key before you release the mouse button.)

Creating polygons

A *polygon* is a closed object that can have any number of sides. Paint-brush lets you create empty and filled polygons. (The border of a filled polygon is drawn with the background color and then filled with the foreground color.) To create a polygon, follow these steps:

1. Select a polygon tool. The mouse pointer changes to a pair of cross hairs.

2. Select the desired foreground color. For a filled polygon, also select a background color.

3. Select the desired line thickness.

4. Move the mouse pointer to the location of the first corner of the border of the polygon you want to draw, and click.

5. Move the mouse pointer to the location of the second corner of the border of the polygon you want to draw, and click. A line appears between the first and second corners.

6. Move the mouse pointer to the location of the next corner of the border of the polygon you want to draw, and click. A line appears between the second and third corners. Repeat this process for each corner of the polygon. Close the polygon by clicking on the starting point.

TERMINAL

Terminal is a telecommunications application that lets one computer exchange information with another, typically via telephone lines.

Starting Terminal

To start Terminal, double-click on the Terminal icon in the Accessories group window. The Terminal window appears, similar to the one shown in Figure 4-15.

FIGURE 4-15. *A new Terminal window.*

Identifying Your Modem

Terminal needs to know what type of modem you are using. To provide this information, follow these steps:

1. Choose Modem Commands from the Settings menu. A dialog box similar to the one shown in Figure 4-16 appears.

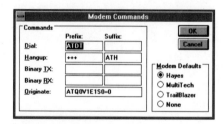

FIGURE 4-16. *The Modem Commands dialog box.*

2. If your modem is listed in the Modem Defaults box, select the option button that corresponds to it. If your modem is not listed, select the Hayes option button.

3. Select the Prefix field of the Dial text box. The letters *ATDT* tell the modem that your phone uses touch-tone dialing. If your phone is rotary, change these letters to *ATDP*. The remaining options in this dialog box are fairly standard, and you probably do not have to change them unless explicitly directed by your modem documentation.

4. Choose OK.

Setting Up Communication Parameters

Before two computers can communicate, they must agree on a set of communication parameters, such as the baud rate and the number of bits. If you access several different computers, each might use a unique set of data communication parameters. To set these up appropriately, follow these steps:

1. Choose Communications from the Settings menu. A dialog box appears, similar to the one shown in Figure 4-17.

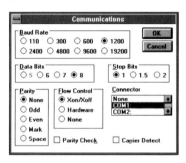

FIGURE 4-17. *The Communications dialog box.*

2. Select a port from the Connector list box and select the data communication settings used by the computer you'll be calling. (You'll need to find this out from the owner of the other computer.)

Setting Up a Phone Number

Specify the phone number of the computer you want to call. To do so, follow these steps:

1. Choose Phone Number from the Settings menu. A dialog box appears, similar to the one shown in Figure 4-18.

FIGURE 4-18. *The Phone Number dialog box.*

2. Type in the number of the computer you intend to call. Type it in as you would dial it. (That is, if you must dial 9 to access an outside line, include the 9 in the Dial text box. If the phone call is long distance, include a 1 and the area code.) You can separate digits with

spaces, parentheses, or hyphens. A comma directs the modem to pause two seconds before continuing dialing. (This is useful to give an office phone system time to connect with an outside line.)

The remaining fields let you tell Terminal what steps to perform if a modem at the other end of the phone line fails to respond in the specified time period:

☐ Timeout If Not Connected In lets you specify how long the computer tries to make a connection. Depending on how far you are calling and on the number of times the phone rings before the other modem answers, you might need to increase the timeout period to 60 seconds or more.

☐ Redial After Timing Out lets you direct Terminal to keep calling until it connects to the other computer.

☐ Signal When Connected directs Terminal to beep to notify you of the connection when it successfully connects to the other computer.

3. After you finish setting options, choose OK.

Saving Communication Information

To save the communication information, choose Save As from the File menu. A dialog box appears, asking you for a filename. Type in a filename, and choose OK. (Unless you specify otherwise, Terminal saves the file with a TRM filename extension.)

Loading Communication Information

To load the communication information back into Terminal, choose Open from the File menu. A dialog box appears, asking what file to load. Type in the filename, and choose OK.

Placing a Phone Call

After you assign the data communication parameters and specify the phone number, you're ready to place a call. To do so, follow these steps:

1. Choose Dial from the Phone menu. A dialog box appears that displays the phone number being called, as well as a countdown of seconds until timeout. If Terminal successfully reaches the other modem, you might hear the two modems exchange tones as they form a connection.

2. When the tones end, press Enter to begin your interaction with the other computer.

3. When you're ready to end the connection, choose Hangup from the Phone menu. Terminal directs your modem to disconnect the call and hangs up the line.

Transferring Files

One of the primary reasons for connecting your computer to another computer is to exchange files. In general, the files you exchange are either text (ASCII files created by a text editor such as Notepad) or binary files such as programs, spreadsheets, or word processing files. Terminal lets you send and receive both kinds of files.

Sending files

To send a file to another computer, follow these steps. (The other computer must be prepared to receive a file.)

1. To send a text file, choose Send Text File from the Transfers menu. To send a binary file, choose Send Binary File from the Transfers menu. A dialog box appears.

2. Type in the name of the file you want to send, and choose OK.

A small status bar that lets you monitor the transfer appears at the bottom of the window.

If Terminal successfully transfers the file, the status bar disappears, and interactive mode resumes. If an error occurs during transmission, a dialog box appears describing the error. You might need to set a Text Transfer or Binary Transfer setting. For more information on these settings, use Terminal's online help, or refer to *Windows for Workgroups Companion.*

Receiving files

To receive a file, follow these steps:

1. To receive a binary file, choose Receive Binary File from the Transfers menu. To receive a text file, choose Receive Text File from the Transfers menu. A dialog box appears, prompting you for the name of the file to receive the text. (You can optionally append the text to an existing file.)

2. Type in the filename, and press Enter. If you're receiving a text file, the text from the remote computer scrolls by on the screen as Terminal captures it in the file. A status bar at the bottom of the window lets you monitor the number of bytes transferred.

3. To end the transmission, click on the Stop button, or choose Stop from Terminal's Transfer menu. If an error occurs, a dialog box describing the error appears.

NOTEPAD

Notepad is a simple text editor that lets you create memos, record notes, or create batch files.

NOTE: *The maximum size of a Notepad document is about 50,000 characters.*

Starting Notepad

To start Notepad, double-click on the Notepad icon in the Accessories group window. A window similar to the one shown in Figure 4-19 appears.

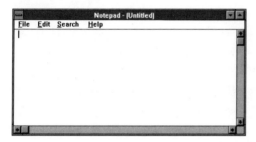

FIGURE 4-19. *A new Notepad window.*

Opening a document

If you want to load an existing document, follow these steps:

1. Choose Open from the File menu. The Open dialog box appears.

2. Type in the name of the document you want to open, or select it (and its directory, if necessary) from the File Name and Directories list boxes. Then choose OK.

Creating a new document

To create a new document, choose New from the File menu. (If you've made changes to the current document, a dialog box appears, asking whether you want to save the changes.)

Saving a document

To save a document, choose Save from the File menu. If this is the first time you've saved the file, the Save As dialog box appears. Simply type in the desired filename. (If a file with that name already exists, a dialog box asks whether you want to replace the existing file. If you choose Yes, the information in the existing file is lost.)

NOTE: *Notepad does not create a backup file for documents. When you save a changed document, the previous document is lost.*

Notepad's File Menu

The following table describes the commands available on the File menu:

Command	Function
New	Creates a new document, first prompting you to save or discard any changes to the current document
Open	Lets you load an existing document
Save	Saves the current document
Save As	Saves the current document with a new name
Print	Prints the document
Page Setup	Lets you define margins as well as insert a header and a footer for each page
Print Setup	Lets you select a printer and change its options
Exit	Closes the Notepad window

Advanced File Editing

The following table describes the commands available on Notepad's Edit menu.

Command	Function
Undo	Cancels the most recent edit
Cut	Deletes the selected text and places it on the Clipboard
Copy	Copies the selected text from the file to the Clipboard
Paste	Copies the contents of the Clipboard to the current document at the cursor's location
Delete	Removes the selected text from the document without placing the text on the Clipboard
Select All	Selects all of the document's text
Time/Date	Inserts the time and date at the cursor location
Word Wrap	Enables word wrapping at the right edge of the window

Notepad Notes

- By default, Notepad does not wrap text, so you must press Enter at the end of each line. (To have Notepad perform word wrapping, choose Word Wrap from the Edit menu.)
- To move through a document, use the arrow, PgUp, PgDn, Home, and End keys, or the vertical and horizontal scroll bars if you're using a mouse.

The following table lists keyboard combinations that help you move around the window:

Keyboard Combination	Function
Home	Moves the cursor to the start of the current line
End	Moves the cursor to the end of the current line
Ctrl+Home	Moves the cursor to the start of the document
Ctrl+End	Moves the cursor to the end of the document
PgUp	Moves the cursor up one page
PgDn	Moves the cursor down one page
Ctrl+right arrow	Moves the cursor right one word
Ctrl+left arrow	Moves the cursor left one word

Moving Text

To move text to a different location in the document, follow these steps:

1. Select the desired text, and choose Cut from the Edit menu. The text disappears from your screen.
2. Move the cursor to where you want the text to reappear, and choose Paste from the Edit menu. The text reappears at the cursor location.

Searching for a Word or a Phrase

To search a document for a word or a phrase, follow these steps.

1. Choose Find from the Search menu. A dialog box appears, similar to the one shown in Figure 4-20.

FIGURE 4-20. *The Find dialog box.*

2. Type in the text you want to find.

3. Select the Match Case check box if Notepad must match uppercase and lowercase letters exactly.

4. Select the direction you want Notepad to search (down toward the end of the document, or up toward the beginning of the document).

If the search is successful, Notepad highlights the found text in the Notepad window. A dialog box informs you if no match occurs. If a match occurs but is *not* the match you want, choose Find Next again. Choose Cancel to close the Find dialog box.

Controlling Notepad's Printed Output

If you choose Page Setup from Notepad's File menu, a dialog box appears, similar to the one shown earlier in Figure 4-2. This dialog box lets you specify a *header* (a line of text that appears at the top of each page) and a *footer* (a line of text that appears at the bottom of each page). This dialog box also lets you specify the page's margin sizes (in inches).

To use the Page Setup dialog box, simply fill in the fields as desired, and then choose OK. By default, the header contains the filename and the footer contains the page number. See the ''Page Setup Options'' section on page 155 for more information about the settings for this dialog box.

Creating a Time-Log Document

If the first line of your document contains the characters *.LOG* (capital letters required), Notepad creates a *time-log document*. Each time you open a time-log document, Notepad appends the current time and date to the document. If you start your new text after the time and date appears, you will have a log of your work. Using the Search menu, you can quickly find a specific day's work.

RECORDER

As you work with Windows on a regular basis, you might find yourself repeatedly opening the same windows and running the same applications. To save time and keystrokes, you can create a Windows *macro*. A Windows macro is a record of the keystrokes and mouse operations required to perform a certain task. The Recorder application lets you record as a macro the keystrokes and mouse operations you perform on a regular basis. When you later need to perform the operation, you can run the macro to perform the steps automatically.

Starting Recorder

To start Recorder, double-click on the Recorder icon in the Accessories group window. A window similar to the one shown in Figure 4-21 appears.

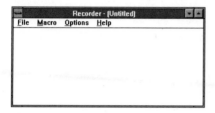

FIGURE 4-21. *A new Recorder window.*

Recording a macro

Normally, you use the mouse to select and choose options. However, this can cause problems in a macro because options such as menus, check boxes, and option buttons aren't always in the same place. To avoid this problem, it's wise to use keyboard combinations rather than the mouse when selecting and choosing options to be recorded as a Windows macro.

To record a Windows macro, follow these steps:

1. Choose Record from the Macro menu. A dialog box similar to the one shown in Figure 4-22 appears.

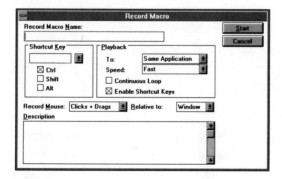

FIGURE 4-22. *The Record Macro dialog box.*

2. Type a descriptive macro name in the Record Macro Name text box, but do *not* press Enter.

3. Move to the Shortcut Key text box, and select a shortcut key combination you want to use to run the macro. For example, if you want the keyboard combination Ctrl+Alt+t to run this macro, type *t* in the Shortcut Key text box, and then select the Ctrl and Alt check boxes. (Do not select a keyboard combination used by the application your macro assists.) If you want to use a special key (such as F1) in the shortcut key combination, select the key from the Shortcut Key drop-down list.

4. The default selections for the remaining options are probably fine. You might want to include a description of the macro in the Description box.

5. Start the application in which the macro is to be used, and then return to the Record Macro dialog box.

6. Choose Start to begin recording. The Recorder window becomes a blinking icon on the desktop to indicate that the recording process has begun.

7. Perform the operations you want to record.

8. After you finish performing the operations you want to record, double-click on the Recorder icon. A dialog box similar to the one shown in Figure 4-23 appears.

FIGURE 4-23. *The Recorder dialog box.*

9. Select Save Macro, and choose OK.

Saving a macro file

To save a macro file on disk, follow these steps:

1. Choose Save As from the File menu. The Save As dialog box appears.

2. Select a drive and directory from the Drives drop-down list and the Directories list box, type a filename into the File Name text box, and choose OK. If a file with that name already exists, Recorder displays a second dialog box asking whether you want to replace the existing file. Choose Yes to replace it or No to cancel the operation.

Loading a macro file

To load a macro file, follow these steps:

1. Choose Open from the File menu. The Open dialog box appears, asking for the name of the macro file.

2. Select a drive and directory from the Drives drop-down list and the Directories list box, type the filename into the File Name text box, and choose OK. Recorder shows the names of each macro in the file.

Running a macro

To run a macro, both Recorder and the macro's application must be running, and the macro file must be loaded. To run a macro, press the macro's shortcut key.

Deleting a macro

To delete a macro, follow these steps:

1. In the Recorder window, select the macro to be deleted.

2. Choose Delete from the Macro menu. A dialog box appears, asking you to confirm the deletion. Choose Yes.

Other Recorder Options

Select or deselect the following commands from the Options menu to control how Recorder operates:

Command	Function
Control+Break Checking	When enabled, allows Ctrl+Break or Ctrl+C to stop a Windows macro
Shortcut Keys	When enabled, allows use of Windows keyboard combinations with macros
Minimize On Use	When enabled, reduces the Recorder to an icon when a Windows macro is run
Preferences	Lets you change several default macro settings

CARDFILE

Cardfile lets you organize information on electronic "index cards." These cards can store a list of names and addresses, birthdays, phone numbers, or virtually any other type of information.

Starting Cardfile

Double-click on the Cardfile icon in the Accessories group window. A window similar to the one shown in Figure 4-24 appears.

To create a new set of cards, choose New from Cardfile's File menu.

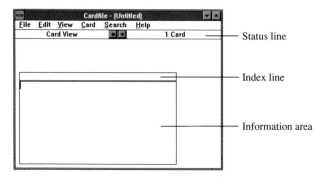

FIGURE 4-24. *A new Cardfile window.*

Assigning an Index

The card's top line is the *index line,* which contains the card's index, or title. To assign an index to a card, follow these steps:

1. Double-click on the card's index line, or select Index from the Edit menu. The Index dialog box appears.

2. Type in a meaningful and—ideally—unique index that describes the card, and then choose OK.

Adding a Card

To add a card, follow these steps:

1. Choose Add from the Card menu. The Add dialog box appears.

2. Type in a meaningful and—ideally—unique index that describes the card's eventual contents, and then choose OK.

3. When Cardfile displays the card, type the card's contents in the information area.

Saving a Cardfile

To save your cards, follow these steps:

1. Choose Save As from the File menu. The Save As dialog box appears.

2. Type in the filename you want. If you specify the name of an existing file, Cardfile displays a dialog box asking whether you want to replace the existing file. Note that if you choose Yes, you lose the information in the existing file.

Loading a Cardfile

To open a file containing previously created cards, follow these steps:

1. Choose Open from the File menu. The Open dialog box appears.
2. Select the drive on which the cards are stored from the Drives drop-down list.
3. Select the directory in which the cards are stored from the Directories list.
4. Type the filename in the File Name text box, or select a file from the list.
5. Choose OK.

The File Menu

The following table describes Cardfile's File menu:

Command	Function
New	Starts a new list of cards, asking whether you want to save changes to the current card list, if any
Open	Lets you load an existing card file
Save	Saves the list of cards to an existing file
Save As	Lets you save a list of cards with a new name
Print	Prints the current card
Print All	Prints every card in the list
Page Setup	Lets you define margins as well as insert a header and a footer for each page
Print Setup	Lets you select a printer and change its options
Merge	Combines the current list of cards with another card list
Exit	Exits Cardfile

Looking Through Your Cards

Cardfile gives you several ways to look through your cards.

Moving forward and backward

To move forward or backward through the list, click on the scroll arrows in the status line, or use one of the key combinations listed in the following table:

Key Combination	Movement
PgUp	Moves backward one card.
PgDn	Moves forward one card.
Ctrl+Home	Moves to the first card in the list.
Ctrl+End	Moves to the last card in the list.
Ctrl+X	Moves to the first card whose index line begins with X. If two or more cards' index lines begin with the same letter or number, press Ctrl+X again to move to the second card, and so on.

Moving with the View menu

Choose List from the View menu to display the cards as a scrollable list of index lines. Cardfile always lists cards alphabetically by index line.

Moving with the Search menu

Cardfile's Search menu provides two ways to search for a card: by index line or by keyword.

Searching by index line To search a set of cards for a specific index line, follow these steps:

1. Choose Go To from the Search menu. The Go To dialog box appears.

2. Type in the desired index line, and choose OK.

If Cardfile locates a matching index line, the matching card appears at the top of the deck. A dialog box informs you if no match is found.

Searching by keyword To search through the text of the cards for a matching word or phrase, follow these steps:

1. Choose Card from the View menu.

2. Choose Find from the Search menu. A dialog box similar to the one shown in Figure 4-25 appears.

FIGURE 4-25. *The Find dialog box.*

3. Type the text you want to search for in the Find What text box.

4. Select Match Case if you want Cardfile to distinguish between uppercase and lowercase letters.

5. Select a direction for the search.

6. Choose Find Next.

7. When your search is complete, choose Cancel in the Find dialog box.

If Cardfile locates a card with matching text, the card containing the match appears at the top of the deck. If—despite the match—this is not the card you want, you can continue the search by choosing Find Next again. A dialog box informs you if no match is found.

Editing Cards

To change a card's contents, follow these steps:

1. Choose Card from the View menu.

2. Move to the desired card.

3. Use the arrow, Delete, and Backspace keys to delete and insert text as necessary.

Undoing an Editing Change

To undo an editing change, choose Undo from the Edit menu. To undo all changes made to the top card since the last save, choose Restore from the Edit menu.

Changing a Card's Index Line

To change a card's index line, follow these steps:

1. Move to the desired card.

2. Double-click on the index line. A dialog box appears, prompting for a new index line.

3. Type in the new index line, and choose OK.

Deleting a Card

To delete a card, follow these steps:

1. Move to the desired card.

2. Choose Delete from the Card menu. A dialog box appears, asking you to confirm the deletion.

3. Choose OK to delete the card, or Cancel to terminate the procedure.

Selecting Text

To select text with the mouse, position the mouse pointer over the start of the text, hold down the left mouse button, and then drag the mouse pointer to the end of the text. Release the left mouse button.

To select text with the keyboard, move the cursor to the beginning of the text, hold down the Shift key, and then use the arrow keys to move the cursor to the end of the text. Release the Shift key.

Copying Text from One Card to Another

To copy text from one card to another, follow these steps:

1. Select the desired text.
2. Choose Copy from the Edit menu.
3. Move to the card to which you want to copy the text. Move the cursor to the location where you want the text.
4. Choose Paste from the Edit menu.

Pasting a Paintbrush Graphic in a Card

To paste a graphic created by Paintbrush in a card, follow these steps:

1. Switch to Paintbrush.
2. Open an existing graphic that you want to paste in a card, or create a new graphic.
3. Use the Pick tool or the Scissors tool to select the graphic.
4. Choose Copy from the Edit menu.
5. Switch to Cardfile.
6. Choose Picture from the Edit menu.
7. Choose Paste from the Edit menu.

To return to editing text, choose Text from the Edit menu.

Linking a Paintbrush Graphic to a Card

When you link a graphic to a card, a copy of the graphic is displayed in the card but the graphic is still stored in its original Paintbrush file. When you make changes to the graphic, these changes appear in every file that contains a link to that graphic.

To link a graphic from Paintbrush, follow these steps:

1. Switch to Paintbrush.

2. Open an existing graphic that you want to link, or create a new graphic.

3. Save your new graphic or any changes you've made to the existing graphic.

4. Use the Pick tool or the Scissors tool to select the graphic.

5. Choose Copy from the Edit menu. A copy of the graphic is placed on the Clipboard.

6. Switch to Cardfile.

7. Open the file containing the card to which you want to link the graphic.

8. Choose Picture from the Edit menu.

9. Choose Paste Link from the Edit menu. Or you can choose the Paste Special command to specify the format of the graphic. If you want to change the format to a bit map or a picture, choose the Paste Special command. If you want the graphic to remain in the Paintbrush Picture format, there is no need for you to choose the Paste Special command.

To return to editing text, choose Text from the Edit menu.

CALCULATOR

The Calculator application acts as a *standard calculator* (for addition, subtraction, multiplication, and division) or as a *scientific calculator* (for trigonometric functions and statistical operations). The first time you use Calculator, the standard calculator, as shown in Figure 4-26, appears.

FIGURE 4-26. *The standard calculator.*

Switching Calculators

To switch between the standard and scientific calculators, choose either Standard or Scientific from the View menu.

Entering Values

To enter values, click on the number buttons or enter numbers with your keyboard.

NOTE: *If you're using the keyboard, you can use the numbers from the top row of the keyboard, or you can use the numbers from the numeric keypad by activating the Num Lock key.*

Using the Standard Calculator

To add, subtract, multiply, or divide two numbers, follow these steps:

1. Enter the first number's digits.
2. Click on the symbol of the desired operation, or press the corresponding key on the keyboard.
3. Enter the second number's digits.
4. Click on the equal sign, or press your keyboard's equal-sign key.

The following table lists calculator buttons, the keyboard equivalent of each button, and the function of each button:

Button	Keyboard Key	Function
C	Esc	Clears the current calculation
CE	Delete	Clears the current value
Back	Backspace or left arrow	Clears the rightmost digit of the current value
MC	Ctrl+L	Clears the contents of memory
MR	Ctrl+R	Recalls the value stored in memory
M+	Ctrl+P	Adds the current value to the value in memory and places the result in memory
MS	Ctrl+M	Stores the current value in memory
+/−	F9	Changes the current value's sign
1/x	R	Calculates the reciprocal of the current value
sqrt	@	Calculates the square root of the current value
%	%	Treats the current value as a percentage
+	+	Adds

(continued)

continued

Button	Keyboard Key	Function
–	–	Subtracts
*	*	Multiplies
/	/	Divides
=	= or Enter	Performs the designated operation on the previous two values; choose again to repeat the operation
.	. or ,	Inserts a decimal point into the current value

Using the Scientific Calculator

To use the scientific calculator, double-click on the Calculator icon in the Accessories group window and choose Scientific from the View menu. The scientific calculator appears, as shown in Figure 4-27.

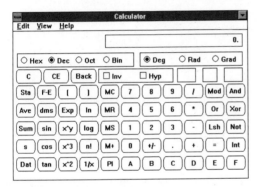

FIGURE 4-27. *The scientific calculator.*

Performing scientific calculations

With the scientific calculator you can work with hexadecimal, decimal, octal, or binary numbers and specify an angle's units of measure in degrees, radians, or gradients.

The following table lists the button, keyboard equivalent, and purpose of each scientific calculator function. (The scientific calculator includes buttons found in the standard calculator.)

Button	Keyboard Key	Function
(	(	Starts a new level of parentheses. The current level of parentheses is shown below the display. The maximum number of levels is 25.
)	)	Closes the current level of parentheses.

(continued)

continued

Button	Keyboard Key	Function
ABCDEF	ABCDEF	Enters the hexadecimal digits A through F. These keys can be used only in the hexadecimal number system.
And	&	Calculates the bitwise exclusive AND of the current value.
Ave	Ctrl+A	Calculates the average of the values in the Statistics Box. Inv+Ave calculates the average of the squares of the values in the Statistics Box.
Bin	F8	Converts to the binary number system.
Byte	F4	Displays the lower 8 bits of the current value.
cos	o	Calculates the cosine of the current value. Inv+cos calculates the arc cosine of the current value. Hyp+cos calculates the hyperbolic cosine of the current value. Inv+Hyp+cos calculates the arc hyperbolic cosine of the current value.
Dat	Ins	Enters the current number in the Statistics Box.
Dec	F6	Converts to the decimal number system.
Deg	F2	Sets trigonometric input for degrees when in decimal mode.
dms	m	Converts the current value to degree-minute-second format. Inv+dms converts the current value to degrees.
DWord	F2	Displays the full 32-bit representation of the current value.
Exp	x	Allows entry of exponential numbers. Exp can be used only in the decimal number system.
F-E	v	Turns scientific notation on or off. F-E can be used only with the decimal number system.
Grad	F4	Sets trigonometric input for gradients when in decimal mode.
Hex	F5	Converts to the hexadecimal number system.
Hyp	h	Sets the hyperbolic function for sin, cos, and tan. These functions automatically turn off the hyperbolic function after a calculation is completed.
Int	;	Displays the integer portion of the current value. Inv+Int displays the fractional portion of the current value.

(continued)

continued

Button	Keyboard Key	Function
Inv	i	Sets the inverse function for sin, cos, tan, PI, x^y, x^2, x^3, ln, log, Ave, Sum, and s. These functions automatically turn off the inverse function after a calculation is completed.
ln	n	Calculates the natural (base *e*) logarithm of the current value. Inv+ln calculates *e* raised to the power of the current value.
log	l	Calculates the base 10 logarithm of the current value. Inv+log calculates 10 raised to the power of the current value.
Lsh	<	Bitwise shifts the current value to the left. Inv+Lsh bitwise shifts the current value right.
Mod	%	Displays the modulus (remainder) of $x \div y$.
n!	!	Calculates the factorial of the current value.
Not	~	Calculates the bitwise inverse of the current value.
PI	p	Displays the value of π. Inv+PI displays $2 \times \pi$.
Rad	F3	Sets trigonometric input for radians when in decimal mode.
Oct	F7	Converts to the octal number system.
Or	¦	Calculates the bitwise OR of the current value.
s	Ctrl+D	Calculates standard deviation with the population parameter as *n–1*. Inv+s calculates standard deviation with the population parameter as *n*.
sin	s	Calculates the sine of the current value. Inv+sin calculates the arc sine of the current value. Hyp+sin calculates the hyperbolic sine of the current value. Inv+Hyp+sin calculates the arc hyperbolic sine of the current value.
Sta	Ctrl+S	Activates the Statistics Box and its associated buttons.
Sum	Ctrl+T	Calculates the sum of the values in the Statistics Box. Inv+Sum calculates the sum of the squares of the values in the Statistics Box.
tan	t	Calculates the tangent of the current value. Inv+tan calculates the arc tangent of the current value. Hyp+tan calculates the hyperbolic tangent of the current value. Inv+Hyp+tan calculates the arc hyperbolic tangent of the current value.

(continued)

continued

Button	Keyboard Key	Function
Word	F3	Displays the lower 16 bits of the current value.
x^2	@	Squares the current value. Inv+x^2 calculates the square root of the current value.
x^3	#	Cubes the current value. Inv+x^3 calculates the cube root of the current value.
x^y	y	Computes x to the yth power. Inv+x^y calculates the yth root of x.
Xor	^	Calculates the bitwise exclusive OR of the current value.

Performing statistical calculations

To perform statistical calculations, double-click on the Calculator icon in the Accessories group window and choose Scientific from the View menu. Choose the scientific calculator's Sta button. Calculator opens a window called the *Statistics Box* which, like any window, you can move to a convenient location on your screen. The Statistics Box appears, as shown in Figure 4-28.

FIGURE 4-28. *The Statistics Box.*

To enter numbers in the Statistics Box, follow these steps:

1. Activate the Calculator window by clicking in it or by choosing the RET button.

2. Enter the desired value.

3. Click on Dat or press the Insert key.

You can enter as many values as you want. After entering all values, you can use the Calculator's statistical functions. If you enter more than six values in the Statistics Box, a vertical scroll bar appears at the right side of the list box. You can use this scroll bar to scroll through the values. The following table describes each Statistics Box button and its purpose:

Button	Function
Ret	Returns to the Calculator window from the Statistics Box
Load	Copies the value selected in the Statistics Box to Calculator
CD	Deletes the value selected in the Statistics Box
CAD	Deletes all values from the Statistics Box

CLOCK

The most straightforward application is Clock. Clock displays the current time and date, using either a digital clock or an analog clock, as shown in Figure 4-29.

FIGURE 4-29. *The Clock window.*

The first time you start Clock, a digital clock appears. To select the analog clock, choose Analog from the Settings menu. To change back to a digital clock, choose Digital from the Settings menu. When you change the clock type, the new type remains in effect—even if you leave Windows—until you specifically change it again.

You can select the clock and then minimize Clock's window to an icon, displaying the current time at the bottom of the screen. This arrangement gives you constant access to the clock but leaves you free to work with other Windows-based applications.

Setting Clock's Font

The digital clock lets you change the font used to display the date and time. To change Clock's font, follow these steps:

1. Choose Set Font from the Settings menu. A dialog box appears, similar to the one shown in Figure 4-30 on the following page.

2. Select the desired font from the Font list box. The Sample box displays several characters drawn in the selected font.

3. Choose OK.

FIGURE 4-30. *The Font dialog box.*

Hiding or Displaying Clock's Title Bar

To hide Clock's title bar, choose No Title from the Settings menu. A faster method of hiding Clock's title bar is to double-click on Clock's window or press Esc. To display Clock's title bar, double-click in Clock's window or press Esc.

Hiding or Displaying the Date

If you choose an analog clock, Clock displays the current date in its title bar. If you choose a digital clock, Clock displays the current date beneath the time. To hide the date, choose Date from the Settings menu. To display the date again, choose Date again from the Settings menu.

Hiding or Displaying Seconds

By default, Clock displays seconds in the current time. To hide the seconds, choose Seconds from the Settings menu. To display seconds again, choose Seconds from the Settings menu.

Setting Clock to be the Topmost Window

Normally, the window of the active application is the topmost window. Clock is special, however—it can be set to remain the topmost window regardless of the active application. To set clock to be the topmost window, choose Always On Top from Clock's Control menu. To restore Clock so that it isn't always the topmost window, choose Always On Top again from Clock's Control menu.

NOTE: *Clock obtains the current time from your computer's internal clock. If the time is incorrect, use the Date/Time option in the Control Panel window to reset it.*

OBJECT PACKAGER

Object Packager is a tool you can use to insert a *package* into a document. A package is an icon that represents an embedded or a linked object. An embedded object is information created in one document and inserted into another document. You can edit an embedded object within that latter document even if you used a different application to create the object. A linked object is a representation of an object that is inserted into a document. The object exists in the original application and, when the object is changed in the original application, the linked object updates to reflect these changes. An object may be a complete document or part of one. For example, both a spreadsheet cell and an entire drawing can be objects.

When you expand the Object Packager icon, a window appears, similar to the one shown in Figure 4-31.

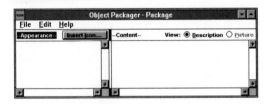

FIGURE 4-31. *The Object Packager window.*

The Object Packager window is split into two smaller windows. The window on the left, the Appearance window, displays the icon that represents the embedded or linked object in the destination document. The window on the right, the Content window, displays a description of the object by default. To see a graphical view of the object, select the Picture option button. To again see the description of the object, select the Description option button. Picture view is available only when the application that created the object is capable of creating linked and embedded objects.

Creating a Packaged Object

To create a packaged object, follow these steps:

1. From the File menu in Object Packager, choose Import. A dialog box appears, similar to the one shown in Figure 4-32 on the following page.

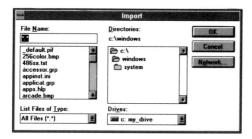

FIGURE 4-32. *The Import dialog box.*

2. In the Import dialog box, select the document you want to package and then choose OK. The icon of the application used to create the file appears in the Appearance window, and the name of the file appears in the Content window.

3. Choose Copy Package from the Edit menu. A copy of the package is placed on the Clipboard.

4. Switch to the application in which you want to place the package. The application must support embedded or linked objects.

5. If applicable, move the cursor to the place where you want the package to appear.

6. Choose Paste from the application's Edit menu.

NOTE: *You can embed or link documents by dragging their icons from File Manager into applications that support embedded or linked objects.*

Creating a Package That Contains Part of a Document

To create a package that contains part of a document, follow these steps:

1. Open the application containing the information you want to package. The application must be able to create objects that can be embedded in or linked to other applications.

2. Select the information you want to package.

3. Choose Copy from the application's Edit menu.

4. Open Object Packager.

5. Select the Content window.

6. Choose Paste from the Edit menu to embed the package, or choose Paste Link to link it.

7. Choose Copy Package from the Edit menu.

8. Switch to the application into which you want to insert the package. The application must support embedded or linked objects.

9. Move the cursor to the place where you want the package to appear.

10. Choose Paste from the application's Edit menu. The package is embedded or linked and appears in the document. Double-click on the package to see its contents.

Selecting a Different Icon

By default, Object Packager uses the icon of the application that created the information for an embedded or linked object. To use a different icon, follow these steps:

1. Choose Insert Icon in the Object Packager window. A dialog box appears, similar to the one shown in Figure 4-33.

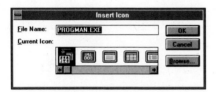

FIGURE 4-33. *The Insert Icon dialog box.*

2. Select an icon from the Current Icon list box.

3. Choose OK. The Insert Icon dialog box closes, and the selected icon appears in the Appearance window.

Creating Your Own Icons

Object Packager also lets you use Paintbrush to create custom icons. To do so, follow these steps:

1. Start Paintbrush and create an image.

2. Use Paintbrush's Pick tool or Scissors tool to select the image.

3. Choose Copy from Paintbrush's Edit menu.

4. Start Object Packager.

5. Select Object Packager's Appearance window.

6. Choose Paste from Object Packager's Edit Menu. The image you created in Paintbrush appears in the Appearance window.

CHARACTER MAP

Character Map is a Windows desktop accessory that lets you copy to the Clipboard characters and symbols from other character sets. You can then paste the characters and symbols from the Clipboard into documents. To start Character Map, double-click on the Character Map icon in the Accessories group window. A window appears, similar to the one shown in Figure 4-34.

FIGURE 4-34. *The Character Map window.*

To copy characters and symbols to the Clipboard using Character Map, follow these steps:

1. Select a font from the Font drop-down list. The characters in Character Map's display change to those of the new font.

2. Select the desired character from Character Map's display by clicking on the character. The selected character appears in an enlarged box, as shown in Figure 4-35.

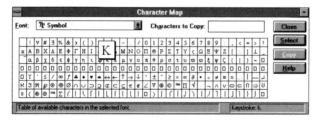

FIGURE 4-35. *The selected character appears in an enlarged box.*

3. Choose Select. The character appears in the Characters To Copy text box.

4. Continue selecting as many characters as you want. After you select all the characters you want, choose Copy to copy the characters to the Clipboard.

5. Switch to the application into which the characters are to be inserted, and choose Paste from the Edit menu.

MEDIA PLAYER

Media Player is a multimedia desktop accessory. If your PC has the appropriate hardware, Media Player lets you play animation, sound, and MIDI sequencer files. To start Media Player, double-click on the Media Player icon in the Accessories group window. A window appears, similar to the one shown in Figure 4-36.

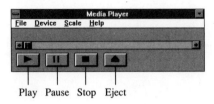

Play   Pause   Stop   Eject

FIGURE 4-36. *The Media Player window.*

Selecting a Media Device

Media Player supports two device types: compound and simple. Compound devices are used to play a specific media file. When you select a compound device, a dialog box appears, prompting you for the name of the file you want to play. Simple devices, on the other hand, play the media information loaded in the device itself. To select a device, follow these steps:

1. Choose the device from the Display menu. (A compound device has an ellipsis [...] after its name.)

2. If you've chosen a compound device, the Open dialog box appears. Type in the name of the media file and choose OK.

NOTE: *The devices listed in the Device menu correspond to MCI (Multimedia Control Interface) devices you have installed in your system. For information on installing MCI devices, see "Managing Device Drivers" in Part III.*

Opening Media Files

If you are using a compound device, you can open and play other media files. To open a media file for a compound device, follow these steps:

1. Choose Open from the File menu. The Open dialog box appears.

2. Type in the name of the media file you want to open, and choose OK.

Selecting a Scale

The Media Player Scale menu lets you display the scale in tracks or time intervals. To change the scale display, choose the option you want from the Scale menu.

Media Player's Buttons

Media Player is similar to a tape recorder, providing Play, Pause, Stop, and Eject buttons. Each works as you would expect it to. The Eject button works only with devices such as a compact disk player that can eject its disk.

Changing the Playback Position

The horizontal scroll bar in the Media Player window controls Media Player's playback position. To select a playback position, drag the scroll box to the location you want, or select the scroll box and use the left or right arrow keys to move it.

SOUND RECORDER

Sound Recorder is a multimedia desktop accessory. If your PC has the appropriate hardware, Sound Recorder lets you play, edit, and record sound files in wave format. To start Sound Recorder, double-click on the Sound Recorder icon in the Accessories group window. A window appears, similar to the one shown in Figure 4-37.

FIGURE 4-37. *The Sound Recorder window.*

Opening a Sound File

To open a sound file for playback or editing, follow these steps:

1. Choose Open from the File menu. The Open dialog box appears.
2. Type in the name of the sound file you want to open, and choose OK.

Sound Recorder's Buttons

Sound Recorder is similar to a tape recorder, providing Rewind, Fast Forward, Play, Stop, and Record buttons. Each works as you would expect it to.

As you play back a sound file, Sound Recorder displays the sound's waveform as if you were viewing the wave on an oscilloscope.

Recording a Sound File

Sound Recorder lets you record up to 60 seconds of sound using a microphone attached to your computer. To record a new sound file, follow these steps:

1. Choose New from the File menu.
2. Choose the Record button.
3. Record up to one minute of sound.
4. Choose Stop.
5. Choose Save As from the File menu. The Save As dialog box appears. Type in a name for the file, and then choose OK.

Adding Sound to an Existing Sound File

To add sound to an existing sound file, follow these steps:

1. Choose Open from the File menu. The Open dialog box appears.
2. Type in the name of the sound file you want to open, and choose OK.
3. Move the scroll box to the location at which you want to insert the new sound.
4. Choose Record.
5. Record the desired sound.
6. Choose Stop.
7. Play the new sound file. If you are satisfied, choose Save from the File menu; otherwise, go back to step 3.

Inserting a Sound File

To insert an existing sound file into your current sound file, follow these steps:

1. Move the scroll box to the location at which you want to insert the sound file.

2. Select Insert File from the Edit menu. The Insert File dialog box appears.

3. Type in the name of the sound file you want to insert, and choose OK.

4. Play your sound file. If you are satisfied, choose Save from the File menu; otherwise, discard the change by choosing Revert from the File menu, and go back to step 1.

Mixing Sound Files

When you mix sound files, the Sound Recorder combines the sounds from two files so that the sounds can be played back simultaneously. To mix two sound files, follow these steps:

1. Load the first sound file into Sound Recorder.

2. Move the scroll box to the location at which you want the mixing to begin.

3. Choose Mix With File from the Edit menu. The Mix With File dialog box appears.

4. Type in the name of the sound file you want to mix, and choose OK.

5. Play your new sound file. If you are satisfied, choose Save from the File menu; otherwise, go back to step 1.

Deleting Part of a Sound File

To delete part of a sound file, follow these steps:

1. Load the sound file you want into Sound Recorder.

2. Move the scroll box to the location you want.

3. To delete all sounds ahead of the location indicated by the scroll box, choose Delete Before Current Position from the Edit menu. To delete all sounds after the scroll box's location, choose Delete After Current Position from the Edit menu.

4. A dialog box asking you to confirm the deletion appears. Choose OK.

5. Play the sound file. If you are satisfied, choose Save from the File menu; otherwise, go back to step 1.

Discarding Changes to a Sound File

If you make changes to a sound file and are unhappy with the results, perform the following steps.

1. Select Revert from the File menu. A dialog box appears, asking you to verify the operation.

2. Select Yes. Sound Recorder restores the sound file to its last saved state.

Changing a Sound's Effects

To increase a sound's volume, choose Increase Volume (by 25%) from the Effects menu. To decrease a sound's volume, choose Decrease Volume from the Effects menu.

To increase the speed at which a sound plays, choose Increase Speed (by 100%) from the Effects menu. To decrease the speed at which a sound plays, choose Decrease Speed from the Effects menu.

To add an echo to a sound, choose Add Echo from the Effects menu.

To reverse a sound, choose Reverse from the Effects menu. Choosing Reverse again restores the sound to its original direction.

CHAT

Chat allows users at two different computers to type an online conversation. Using Chat is similar to using a phone. The words typed by each of the users appear immediately on both screens. Using Chat, you can call another user or another user can call you at any time.

Answering and Ending a Call

When a user calls you, Windows displays the Chat icon at the bottom of your screen with the name of the computer calling you beneath the icon.

If you have sound enabled for Chat, your screen will also periodically beep as the phone "rings." To answer the call, double-click on the icon. (If the Chat window is open when someone calls, answer by choosing the toolbar's Answer button.) Windows displays the Chat window, shown in Figure 4-38 on the following page, just as if you had double-clicked on the Chat icon in the Accessories group window.

If you do not answer a call, the caller will eventually "hang up."

After you answer the call, the two computers are connected. To begin your conversation, simply start typing. The text you type appears in the top message window on your screen and in the bottom message window on the screen of the person you are calling.

To end a call, choose the Hang Up button.

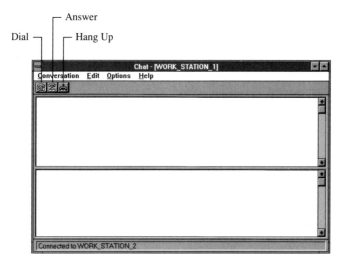

FIGURE 4-38. *The Chat window.*

Making a Call

To call another user, follow these steps:

1. Choose the toolbar's Dial button. Chat displays a Select Computer dialog box, similar to the one shown in Figure 4-39.

2. In the Computers list box, select the computer of the user you want to call. (The list box contains both workgroup names and computer names.) If you want to call someone you've called before, choose the computer from the Computer Name drop-down list.

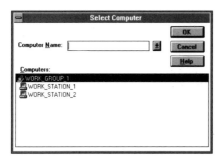

FIGURE 4-39. *The Select Computer dialog box.*

3. Choose OK. The status bar will display messages letting you know when Chat is attempting to connect and when the connection is successful. After you have connected, begin your conversation.

Cutting and Pasting Message Text

Chat lets you copy the current contents of the Clipboard to the Chat window, or cut or copy message text from the Chat window to the Clipboard. To perform cut and paste operations, use the Edit menu commands, described in the following list:

Command	Function
Cut	Cuts selected text to the Clipboard
Copy	Copies selected text to the Clipboard
Paste	Copies the contents of the Clipboard to the Chat window, making the contents visible to the connected user
Select All	Selects all the text in the current message window

Scrolling Through Message Text

Chat lets you scroll through the text you have sent or received by using the arrow keys or the vertical scroll bar that appears next to each message window.

Customizing Chat

The commands on the Options menu let you customize Chat. You can organize Chat's message windows, change the font and screen color in the message window that displays what you type, and toggle the display of the toolbar and status bar and the use of sound.

Organizing message windows

Chat lets you display the two message windows one on top of the other, or side by side. To change the window orientation, follow these steps:

1. Choose Preferences from the Options menu. Chat displays the Preferences dialog box, shown in Figure 4-40.

FIGURE 4-40. *The Preferences dialog box.*

2. Select the window orientation you want in the Window Style box.

3. Choose OK.

Managing message fonts

Chat lets you select the font used for your messages. You can also choose the font's color. To select a font and its color, follow these steps:

1. Choose Font from the Options menu. Chat displays the Font dialog box, shown in Figure 4-41.

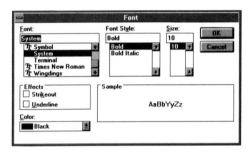

FIGURE 4-41. *The Font dialog box.*

2. Select the desired font, font style, and font size.

3. Select one or both of the check boxes in the Effects box. Select the Strikeout check box to place a horizontal line through the message text. Select the Underline check box to underline the message text.

4. Choose the font color from the Color drop-down list. This color will be visible both to you and to the person with whom you are conversing.

5. Choose OK.

Selecting a background color

To select the background color on which your messages appear both to you and to the person with whom you are conversing, follow these steps:

1. Choose Background Color from the Options menu. Chat displays the Color dialog box, shown in Figure 4-42.

To select one of the colors in the Basic Colors section, click on the desired color. Choose OK. Chat then uses as its background color the solid color closest to the color you chose.

Because the Color dialog box was derived from the Control Panel's Color dialog box (discussed in the "Changing Screen Colors" section in Part III), it displays the Custom Colors boxes and the Define Custom Colors button. Chat, however, can't use custom colors, so these fields aren't available.

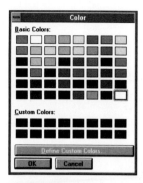

FIGURE 4-42. *The Color dialog box.*

Controlling the toolbar display

Chat lets you turn the toolbar display on or off. To toggle the current toolbar setting, choose Toolbar from the Options menu. If a check mark precedes the menu command, the toolbar is displayed.

Controlling the status bar display

Chat lets you turn the status bar display on or off. To toggle the current status bar setting, choose Status Bar from the Options menu. If a check mark precedes the menu command, the status bar is displayed.

Controlling the phone ring

Chat lets you turn the use of sound (the ringing phone) on or off. To toggle the current sound setting, choose Sound from the Options menu. If a check mark precedes the menu command, sound is on.

WINMETER

If you're running Windows for Workgroups in 386 enhanced mode, remote programs can access your computer's resources. Because you also use those resources for your programs, it may be difficult for you to determine which programs are consuming your system's processing time. WinMeter displays a graph of your computer's processor utilization. When you start WinMeter, your screen displays a window similar to the one shown in Figure 4-43 on the following page.

The horizontal lines correspond to processor utilization, as a percentage from 0 through 100. WinMeter displays the amount of processor time consumed by local applications and by remote programs, using a different color for each. When the WinMeter window is enlarged, it displays the times at which the measurements were taken. WinMeter lets you select a time interval from 5 seconds through 10 minutes.

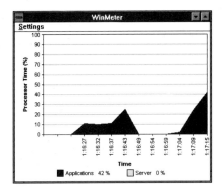

FIGURE 4-43. *The WinMeter window.*

NOTE: *If you minimize WinMeter to an icon, the icon will continue to display the system utilization.*

Selecting the Measurement Interval

To select a measurement interval, choose the interval time you want from the Settings menu. WinMeter will start using the new interval immediately.

Turning the Legend Display On or Off

The WinMeter legend lets you know which color is used for local applications and which is used for remote applications. WinMeter lets you turn the display of the legend on or off. To control the legend display, choose the Show Legend command from the Settings menu. The command works as a toggle, turning the legend display on or off. If the command is preceded by a check mark, WinMeter displays the legend.

Controlling WinMeter Colors

To change the colors WinMeter uses to display local and remote utilization, follow these steps:

1. Choose either Application Color or Server Color from the Settings menu. WinMeter displays the Color dialog box, shown in Figure 4-44.

The Color dialog box was derived from the Control Panel's Color dialog box, discussed in the "Changing Screen Colors" section in Part III. To select one of the colors in the Basic Colors section, click on the desired color. Choose OK. To create a custom color, refer to the discussion in Part III.

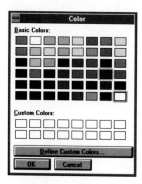

FIGURE 4-44. *The Color dialog box.*

Controlling the Title Bar Display

WinMeter lets you show or hide the title bar that appears at the top of
its window. To hide the title bar, either double-click in the WinMeter
window or choose Hide Title Bar from the Settings menu. To redisplay
the title bar, double-click in the WinMeter window.

NET WATCHER

If you are running Windows for Workgroups in 386 enhanced mode and
have one or more shared directories on your computer, you can use the
Net Watcher accessory to view and control which users in your
workgroup are currently using the directories and which files the users
have open. You can also view and control which users are connected to
a printer that you share. To start Net Watcher, double-click on the Net
Watcher icon in the Accessories group window. A window similar to the
one in Figure 4-45 on the following page appears. The Net Watcher
window has two panes. The pane on the left shows the computers currently connected to your system. The pane on the right shows the directories and printers to which the selected computer is connected and the
files that are open.

Net Watcher precedes each item in the right pane of the window with
one or two icons. The first icon specifies the type of item the user is
using and can be a shared directory icon, a document icon, or a printer
icon. The second icon specifies whether the item is read-only (a glasses
icon) or read-write (a pencil icon).

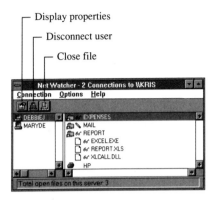

FIGURE 4-45. *The Net Watcher window.*

Viewing User Details

To display additional details about a user and his or her connections to
your computer, either double-click on the user's computer name or select
the user's computer name in the Net Watcher window and click on the
Display Properties button on the toolbar. Net Watcher displays a Properties dialog box similar to the one shown in Figure 4-46. Choose OK
when you're done.

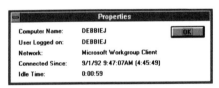

FIGURE 4-46. *The Properties dialog box.*

Disconnecting a User

Net Watcher lets you disconnect any user who is connected to your computer. To disconnect a user, follow these steps:

1. Select the user's computer name.

2. Click on the Disconnect User button on the toolbar. Net Watcher displays a dialog box asking you to verify the disconnect operation.

3. Choose Yes.

Closing a File

To close a file currently open and being used by a user connected to
your computer, follow these steps:

1. Select the desired file.

2. Click on the Close File button on the toolbar. Net Watcher displays a dialog box asking you to verify the Close File operation.

3. Choose Yes.

Controlling the Net Watcher Display

Net Watcher lets you modify many aspects of its display.

Controlling the toolbar display

Net Watcher lets you toggle on or off the display of its toolbar by choosing Toolbar from the Options menu. If a check mark precedes the Toolbar command, Net Watcher displays the toolbar; otherwise, it hides the toolbar.

Controlling the status bar display

Net Watcher lets you toggle on or off the display of its status bar by choosing Status Bar from the Options menu. If a check mark precedes the Status Bar command, Net Watcher displays the status bar; otherwise, it hides the status bar. Net Watcher uses the status bar to display the names of selected directories and to explain menu options.

Refreshing the screen display

Because users in your workgroup can connect to or disconnect from your shared directories or printers at any time, the information in the Net Watcher window might become outdated. To update the information, either press the F5 key or choose Refresh from the Options menu.

Sizing the Net Watcher panes

By default, Net Watcher displays two panes. The pane on the left contains the names of connected computers and the pane on the right contains the list of directories, printers, and files that the selected computer is using. To change the size of these panes, position the mouse pointer over the split bar between the panes and drag the bar to the position you want.

PART V

Games

Windows provides two computer games: Solitaire and Minesweeper. To select a game, open the Games group in the Program Manager window. The Games group window appears, similar to the one shown in Figure 5-1.

FIGURE 5-1. *The Games group window.*

PLAYING SOLITAIRE

To play Solitaire, double-click on the Solitaire icon in the Games group window. A new window appears, similar to the one shown in Figure 5-2.

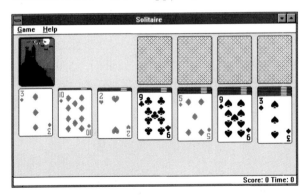

FIGURE 5-2. *The Solitaire window.*

The goal of Solitaire is to build four stacks of cards—one for each suit. The cards are stacked in order of rank, from ace to king, along the top of the Solitaire window.

The seven lower columns of cards begin with one card in column 1, two cards in column 2, and so on up to seven cards in column 7. The top card of each column is placed face up, and the unexposed cards below it are placed face down.

Each card has a rank. Aces have the lowest rank and kings have the highest rank. A card can be moved from one column to another, as long as the top card of the column you're moving to is ranked one card higher than the card you're placing and is a different color. For example, the six of hearts could be moved from one column to be placed on top of the seven of clubs in another column. Whenever a face-down card in one of the columns is exposed, the card can be turned face up.

In the same manner, a sequence of upturned cards can be moved to another column, as long as the top card of the other column has a higher rank and is a different color than the bottom card of the sequence.

Kings and aces are special. Kings can be moved to vacated columns in the lower columns, whereas aces can be moved to the vacant stacks located in the upper right corner of the Solitaire window. Top cards of the lower columns can also be moved to these upper stacks, as long as the top card of the lower stack has the next highest rank and is of the same suit. For example, the two of hearts can be moved up onto the ace of hearts.

A deck of cards (stacked face down), located in the upper left corner of the Solitaire window, is turned over either one or three at a time, depending on the option you've chosen. The top card can be moved to either one of the lower columns or one of the upper stacks, as long as the rules of rank and color are satisfied. When all cards in this deck are turned over, most likely you should turn the deck face down again (depending on what options you've chosen). Click on the empty box to do so and begin turning over cards from this deck again.

Working with Cards

Moving a card is easy—simply use the mouse to drag the card to its new position. To turn a card over, simply click on the card.

Selecting a Card Design

Solitaire lets you choose the appearance of the back of your cards. To do so, use the following steps.

1. Choose Deck from the Game menu. A dialog box appears, displaying sample card backs, as shown in Figure 5-3.

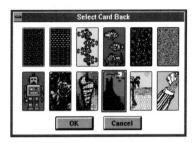

FIGURE 5-3. *Solitaire's available card backs.*

2. Select the desired card back and then choose OK.

Starting a New Game

To start a new game, choose Deal from the Game menu. Solitaire shuffles the cards and deals.

Options

In addition to straight Solitaire, you can select Standard or Vegas scoring rules. To select the scoring rules, choose Options from the Game menu. A dialog box similar to the one shown in Figure 5-4 appears.

FIGURE 5-4. *The Options dialog box.*

The Draw option buttons control how Solitaire deals cards from the available card pile: either one card at a time, or three cards at a time. The Timed Game check box lets you turn Solitaire's game timer on or off. The Status Bar check box lets you turn on or off the status bar Solitaire uses to display the score and timer. The Outline Dragging check box controls whether the entire card or only the card's outline is displayed as you drag it. The Keep Score check box, which is available only with Vegas scoring, lets you keep a running score from game to game.

In Standard scoring, Solitaire scores the game as follows:

- +5 points for any card moved from the deck to a card column
- +10 points for any card played onto a suit stack
- −15 points for moving a card from a suit stack to a card column
- −20 points for each pass, after three passes, with the Draw Three option
- −100 points for each pass, after one pass, with the Draw One option

In Vegas scoring, Solitaire scores the game as follows:

- Your initial wager is $52.
- You win $5 for each card you place in a suit stack.
- You get only one pass through the card deck with the Draw One option.
- You get only three passes through the card deck with the Draw Three option.

PLAYING MINESWEEPER

Minesweeper is a board game that combines chance and skill. To play Minesweeper, double-click on the Minesweeper icon in the Games group window. A window similar to the one shown in Figure 5-5 appears.

FIGURE 5-5. *The Minesweeper game board.*

The board, initially an 8-by-8 grid, contains 10 mines. Your goal is to identify the location of each mine.

To begin, click on a square. If the square contains a mine, the location of each mine is revealed and the game is over, as shown in Figure 5-6 on the following page.

FIGURE 5-6. *An unsuccessful game.*

If the square doesn't contain a mine, a number appears in the square, as shown in Figure 5-7.

FIGURE 5-7. *An uncovered square.*

Each square is surrounded by up to eight other squares. The number Minesweeper displays in an uncovered square indicates the number of mines contained in the squares surrounding the uncovered square. For example, there are two mines hidden in the eight squares that surround the uncovered square in Figure 5-7. By combining your knowledge about the number of mines contained in the surrounding squares, you can narrow down the squares that you think contain mines. Do not click on a square that you think contains a mine. Doing so would explode the mine and end the game. Instead, use the right mouse button to click on the square. This marks the square with a flag, as shown in Figure 5-8.

FIGURE 5-8. *Marking a suspected mine location.*

If you are not sure whether a square contains a mine, you can click twice on the square using the right mouse button. A question mark appears in the square. After you make other moves, you can click twice on the square with the right mouse button to change the question mark into a flag if you think the square contains a mine, or you can click on the square with the left mouse button to uncover it.

Minesweeper has four levels:

Beginner	64 squares, 10 mines
Intermediate	256 squares, 40 mines
Expert	480 squares, 99 mines
Custom	User-defined

Choose the level you want from the Game menu.

Minesweeper keeps track of the fastest time at each level. If you have the fastest time for your level, Minesweeper displays a dialog box asking you to type in your name.

Installing Windows for Workgroups

This section helps you if you need to install Windows for Workgroups. Before you can continue, note that you must be using MS-DOS version 3.3 or later. The instructions throughout this book assume you are using MS-DOS 5 or later.

HARDWARE REQUIREMENTS FOR WINDOWS FOR WORKGROUPS

You can use Windows for Workgroups in either of two modes: 386 enhanced mode and standard mode. When you run it in 386 enhanced mode, you can share your directories and printers and connect to other people's directories and printers. With standard mode, you can only connect to other resources. The two modes have most hardware requirements in common:

- An EGA, VGA, Super VGA, 8514/A, Hercules graphics card, or compatible graphics adapter and monitor (VGA or better resolution recommended)
- A Windows-compatible network adapter card
- 640 KB conventional memory
- At least 9.5 MB free hard-disk space (14 MB recommended)
- At least one floppy-disk drive
- A mouse (not necessary, but highly recommended)

To use Windows for Workgroups in 386 enhanced mode, you also need

- An IBM-PC–compatible computer with an 80386SX or higher microprocessor
- 3 MB extended memory

To use Windows for Workgroups in standard mode, you also need

- An IBM-PC–compatible computer with an 80286 or higher microprocessor
- 256 KB extended memory (1024 KB recommended)

INSTALLING WINDOWS

To begin installation, place Windows' installation floppy disk 1 in drive A, and use the following command to change to drive A:

```
C:\>A: <Enter>
```

Then use the following command to run Setup:

```
A:\>SETUP <Enter>
```

Read the information that appears about installing Windows, and press Enter to continue. Setup then asks whether you want to perform an Express Setup or a Custom Setup. Unless you're an experienced computer user, press Enter to choose Express Setup.

If you're upgrading from Windows version 3.0 or 3.1, Setup prompts you for the name of the directory to which you want to install Windows for Workgroups. Simply press Enter to accept the suggested directory. If you're installing Windows for the first time, the Express setup automatically uses the WINDOWS directory.

Next Setup begins copying files onto your hard disk, occasionally asking you to insert the other installation disks. Insert each disk and press Enter as directed.

Eventually a dialog box appears, similar to the one shown in Figure A-1. Type your name, your company's name, the name you want to give your computer, and your workgroup's name into the text boxes, and then choose OK. Setup asks you to confirm your choices and then continues installing Windows.

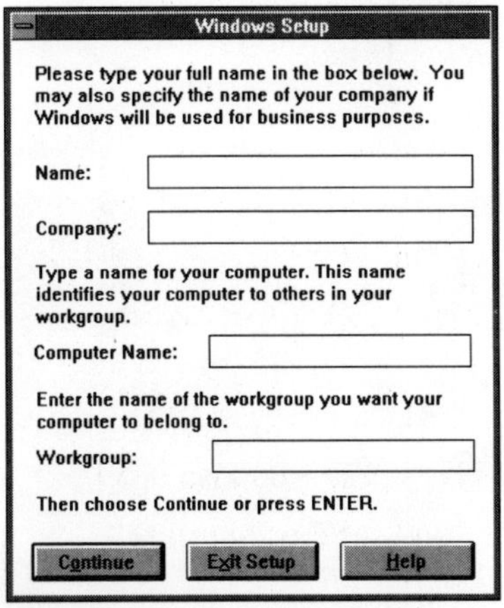

FIGURE A-1. *Setup asks you to type your name, your company's name, your computer's name, and your workgroup's name.*

Selecting a Printer

As the installation continues, Setup asks you to select a printer. Printer selection is actually a two-step process: First you select the printer attached to your computer, and then you configure it. This section describes this process.

A dialog box appears, similar to the one shown in Figure A-2, requesting that you select a printer.

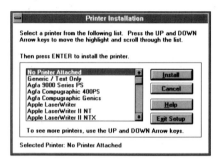

FIGURE A-2. *Select your printer from the Printer Installation dialog box.*

1. Use the arrow keys to scroll through the printer list and select your printer. (To speed up this process, type the first letter of your printer's name.) If your printer's name does not appear, highlight No Printer Attached and later use the Control Panel to install the printer.

2. Choose Install.

3. Setup might ask you to insert another disk. Do so and press Enter.

After you've selected a printer, a dialog box appears, asking you to select the port to which the printer is attached, as shown in Figure A-3. Select a port from the list box and then choose Install.

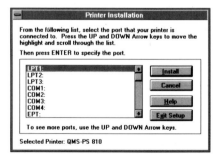

FIGURE A-3. *Select a port from the Printer Installation dialog box.*

Selecting a Network Adapter

Setup then displays the Install New Network Adapter dialog box, shown in Figure A-4.

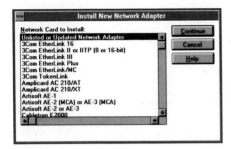

FIGURE A-4. *The Install New Network Adapter dialog box.*

Select your network adapter type and then choose Continue. Setup displays a dialog box that shows the adapter's hardware settings. You can choose the Protocol button in the dialog box to specify the protocol the network uses to transfer information from one computer to another.

Choose Continue to continue the installation. Setup immediately displays the Other Networks dialog box, which lets you specify any other networks to which your computer is connected. To specify a network, select the network's name from the Available Network Types list box and then choose Add. The name will appear in the Other Networks In Use list box. Choose Continue.

Setting Up Applications

After you select and configure your printer and network, Setup begins searching your hard disk for applications. A dialog box appears, similar to the one shown in Figure A-5.

FIGURE A-5. *The Windows Setup dialog box.*

If Setup finds an application it can't identify, it asks you to select the application, as shown in Figure A-6.

FIGURE A-6. *Setup asks you to select the name of an application it can't identify.*

Select the application's name and then choose OK. After it finishes searching, Setup installs the applications it found.

After installing applications, Setup displays a dialog box, similar to the one shown in Figure A-7, asking whether you want to run the Windows tutorial. The tutorial introduces you to Windows and mouse operations.

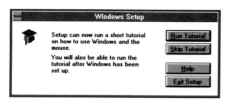

FIGURE A-7. *Setup asks whether you want to run the tutorial.*

If you are new to Windows, choose Run Tutorial to run the tutorial. If you don't want to run the tutorial, choose Skip Tutorial. Setup continues the installation. Part I of this reference shows you how to run the tutorial at a later time from within Windows.

Completing the Windows Installation

The Windows installation is now complete. Setup displays a dialog box, similar to the one shown in Figure A-8.

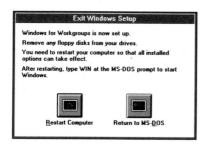

FIGURE A-8. *The Exit Windows Setup dialog box.*

Choose the Reboot button. After your computer restarts, type *win* to start Windows for Workgroups.

TROUBLESHOOTING YOUR NETWORK CONNECTION

When you select a network adapter during the Windows installation, Setup creates a file in the Windows directory named PROTOCOL.INI. The file specifies information about your network card, including the base I/O port address, base memory address, and interrupt number. The base I/O port address identifies the portion of memory that the adapter uses to communicate with the computer. The base memory address identifies the portion of memory that the adapter uses when it receives and sends information across the network. The interrupt number is the value the adapter uses to get the computer's attention. The values Setup places in PROTOCOL.INI are the values most often used for your network card. However, the values might not match those currently selected for your adapter. If you cannot access the network, note your adapter's current settings (typically set by dip switches or jumpers on the adapter) and choose the Adapters button in the Control Panel's Network Adapters dialog box. Then choose the Setup button and modify the values as necessary. Windows updates the PROTOCOL.INI file for you.

WHICH MODE IS RIGHT FOR YOU?

Windows runs in one of two modes: standard and 386 enhanced mode. Each mode provides Windows with a certain degree of power. The following paragraphs provide a brief description of each mode and its capabilities.

Standard Mode

Windows for Workgroups automatically runs in standard mode on computers that use the Intel 80286 microprocessor (or an equivalent microprocessor) and have 640 KB of conventional memory and at least 256 KB of extended memory. Standard mode lets you start and run as many Windows-based applications as you'd like, limited by the amount of your computer's available memory. You can run applications designed for MS-DOS as well, but applications designed for MS-DOS must use the full screen and run in the foreground only.

Standard mode also lets you connect to any directory or printer in your workgroup. However, you can't share your own directories and printers.

386 Enhanced Mode

386 enhanced mode is the most powerful operating mode available with Windows. Windows for Workgroups automatically runs in 386 enhanced mode on computers with an 80386SX, 80386, i486SX, or i486 microprocessor (or equivalent microprocessors) with 640 KB of conventional memory and at least 3072 KB of extended memory.

In 386 enhanced mode, Windows can treat free space on your hard drive as extra memory. (This is known as *virtual memory*.) In 386 enhanced mode, you can start and run as many Windows-based applications as you'd like, limited by the amount of your computer's available memory. 386 enhanced mode also lets applications designed for MS-DOS use the full screen or run in a window. With 386 enhanced mode, you can share your directories and printers with other people in your workgroup in addition to connecting to other shared resources.

Fundamental Keys in Windows

In Windows you can perform a number of tasks with a few simple key combinations. Figure B-1 lists the key combinations you typically use within a window.

Key(s)	Function
Alt+Spacebar	Opens an application window's Control menu
Alt+Hyphen	Opens a document window's Control menu
Alt+F4	Closes the active application window
Ctrl+F4	Closes the active group or document window
Alt+Esc	Selects the next application window or icon
Alt+Tab	Performs fast switching between applications
Ctrl+Tab	Activates the next group or document window
Ctrl+Esc	Opens the Task List
Alt+Print Screen	Copies an image of the active window to the Clipboard
Print Screen	Copies the current screen image to the Clipboard
F1	Activates online help
Shift+F1	Activates context-sensitive help on a specific command or screen element (available only with some applications designed for Windows)

FIGURE B-1. *Fundamental key combinations used in windows.* *(continued)*

continued

Key(s)	Function
Ctrl+F6	Selects the next document or group icon
Alt+X	Opens the menu denoted by X (where X is the underlined letter in the menu name)
F10	Selects the first menu on the menu bar

Figure B-2 lists key combinations you commonly use within a dialog box.

Key(s)	Function
Alt+F4 or Esc	Cancels a dialog box
Shift+Tab	Moves to the previous field
Tab	Moves to the next field
Alt+X	Selects the element noted by X (where X is the underlined letter on screen)
Alt+down arrow	Opens the selected drop-down list
Alt+up arrow	Closes a drop-down list, transferring the selected item to the text box portion of the drop-down list
Home	Moves to the first character in a text box
End	Moves to the last character in a text box
Enter	Executes the command corresponding to the dialog box's default button
Spacebar	Selects or deselects a check box

FIGURE B-2. *Fundamental key combinations used in dialog boxes.*

Index

Special Characters

? (question mark), 114, 116
1½ space command, 164
386 enhanced mode
  handling device contention, 148–49
  memory, 230
  PIF options, 115–19
  scheduling options, 149
  swap files, 150–51

A

About command, 10, 45
accessing. *See also* opening
  bookmarks, 14
  definitions, 11
  help, 10–11
  network drives, 42–43
  other networks, 145–46
  remote ClipBooks, 96–97
  schedules, 88–90
  windows, 4
adding
  applications to groups, 19–20, 35
  appointments, 71–72, 77–78
  buttons or separators to toolbar, 26–27
  cards, 188
  device drivers, 151–52
  documents to groups, 35
  fonts, 124
  groups, 18–19
  items to group windows, 35
  printers, 101, 137–38
  sound, 147–48
address books. *See* Mail application,
  address books
Airbrush tool, 169, 172
alignment. *See also* Justified command
  paragraphs, 164, 167
  text, 163
Always Warn option, 148
animation. *See* Media Player
annotating, help text, 15–16

applications
  background execution, 149
  command line, 114, 116
  deleting from groups, 20
  description, changing, 21
  desktop (*see* desktop accessories)
  display options
    386 enhanced mode, 116–19
    standard mode, 114–15
  embedding files in (*see* Object Packager)
  exiting (*see* Exit command; exiting)
  filename extensions, 37
  groups (*see* Program Manager)
  icons, 19, 22
  memory options
    386 enhanced mode, 116–19
    standard mode, 114–15
  moving between groups, 20
  MS-DOS–based
    386 enhanced mode, 115–19, 148–51
    creating PIFs for, 112–19
    running, 112–13
  multiple
    386 enhanced mode scheduling
      options, 149
    device contention, 148–49
    Task List, 112
  name, 37, 114
  non-Windows (*see* applications,
    MS-DOS–based)
  pathname, 114, 115
  preventing switching, 115, 117
  running
    386 enhanced mode, 148–51
    automatically at startup, 21
    directory window, 30
    minimized, 20
    MS-DOS–based applications (*see*
      applications, MS-DOS–based)
    performance, 144
    Task List, 112

Kris Jamsa

Kris Jamsa is the author of over 40 computer books on a wide range of topics, including MS-DOS, hard disk management, MS-DOS batch files, Microsoft Windows, graphics, programming languages, Word-Perfect, and WordPerfect for Windows. Many of his books have appeared on bestseller lists across the country, and collectively they have sold over one million copies.

Jamsa grew up in Seattle and moved to Phoenix, Arizona, for high school. He received his bachelor's degree in computer science from the United States Air Force Academy in 1983. After graduation, Jamsa worked in Las Vegas as a VAX/VMS system manager for the Air Force. In 1986 he received his master's degree in computer science from the University of Nevada at Las Vegas. Jamsa left the Air Force in 1988 to write full time. He is currently a Ph.D. candidate at Arizona State University, researching multiprocessor operating systems.

He lives in Las Vegas with his wife, Debbie, their daughters, Stephanie and Kellie, and Happy, their dalmatian puppy.